MARIOLOGICAL
STUDIES IN HONOR OF
Our Lady of Guadalupe

3

Mariological Studies in Honor of
Our Lady of Guadalupe

Shrine of Our Lady of Guadalupe
La Crosse, Wisconsin, U.S.A.

edited by
FR. PETER DAMIAN M. FEHLNER, F.I.

ACADEMY OF THE IMMACULATE
New Bedford, MA

Mariological Studies in Honor of Our Lady of Guadalupe - 3
is a book prepared for publication by
the Academy of the Immaculate
[academyoftheimmaculate.com],
POB 3003, New Bedford, MA 02741-3003

Cum Permissu Superiorum

September 12, 2016

The permission of the superiors is a declaration of the Roman Catholic Church that a work is free from error in matters of faith and morals; but in no way does it imply that she endorses the contents of the book.

ISBN: 978-1-60114-075-3

COVER
photo credit: Fr. Lawrence Lew, O.P.
graphic designer: Mary Flannery, Flannery Studios

PRINTED IN THE UNITED STATES OF AMERICA

Table of Contents

INTRODUCTION

At first glance, the collected chapters in this volume seem unrelated to one another. But this is only a superficial impression. Each essay contributes in a unique way to our understanding of diverse aspects of the Immaculate Mother's maternal Mediation, a mediation rooted in the mystery of the Immaculate Conception, and a doctrine of the Church presently under sharp attack by adversaries. Precisely this very positive approach, resting on a renewal of our faith, makes the approach attractive and reasonable in the face of ill-founded falsehoods. Mary, as maternal Mediatrix, bringing Jesus to us and us to Jesus, has prime importance today in every aspect of our lives here below as we prepare for heaven and eternal bliss in the Communion of Saints.

The first essay is a very well done reflection on the reaffirmation of the traditional doctrine of Marian Mediation as taught by the Church. This reaffirmation, also in the doctrinal constitution on the mystery of the Church of Vatican II, has since also been reaffirmed in the teaching of St. Pope John Paul II and Pope Benedict XVI. Gloria Falcão Dodd, in her essay: *Mary as Mediatrix in* Lumen Gentium *62. In continuity with Guadalupe, Fatima and St. Maximilian Kolbe*, shows that, far from being a pious opinion, this reaffirmation is, in fact, in continuity with our Lady's work of mediation at such extraordinary places as Guadalupe and Fatima and in the work to convert the entire human family to Jesus through the maternal Mediation of Mary: who brings Jesus to us as her Son and us to Him as adopted children. The entire study is well documented with footnotes and provides a good list of further readings in English. No doubt that Professor Dodd is a very competent scholar and student of Mary, but she also has a certain ease in enabling the ordinary reader to understand the fruit of her research.

The second essay is by the well known Msgr. Charles M. Mangan. The title of his study: *Our Lady of Fatima's Summons to Sacrifice for Sinners as Exemplified by St. Maximilian Maria Kolbe*, summarizes what he wishes to call to the attention of the simple and the scholarly. The summons to sacrifice for sinners is without doubt an extension of Mary's maternal Mediation, while the response of St. Maximilian to the same call centers on the maternal Mediation of Mary as founded in the mystery of the Immaculate Conception. Only by bringing these truths together will the summons and its execution succeed in the conversion and sanctification of sinners.

Jonathan Fleischmann, in our third essay entitled *Vertex of Love*, taken from the writings of St. Maximilian, turns our attention to some very important aspects, little known in the English speaking part of the globe, of St. Maximilian's teaching about Mary's maternal Mediation: how, as rooted in the mystery of the Immaculate Conception, she is intimately united to the Immaculate of Heaven, the Holy Spirit. In such an exalted position, she forms the vertex of love with the Holy Spirit: all the love of heaven represented by the Holy Spirit and all the love of creation represented by the Mother of God. Here we see how her Motherhood, as divine and as spiritual, is heart of that maternal Mediation. As Mother of God and of Christ's brothers and sisters, she makes possible the unique instrument used by Jesus in the realization of the divine plan of salvation.

Finally, Fr. Giacinto Marie Dagasse, in the very long but hardly boring, concluding essay, demonstrates to the English speaking world a relatively new way of appreciating Our Lady, not as someone to be treated impersonally as an object of study, but as one to be known and loved personally, from whom we learn about the mysteries of Jesus and the salvation awaiting us in heaven. I say relatively new, since the essence of this method of learning under the tutelage or mediation of Mary was known to the ancients such as St. Bonaventure.

First Fr. Giacinto selects a revealed account, e.g., of the Annunciation to which he attaches what he calls Marian commentaries, that is, the truths made known by the conversation between Mary and the Archangel waiting on her. Next, he selects words to be studied from this passage as means of deeper understanding: words he understands as particularly important for revealing the mysteries in this commentary and how mistakes were made, and still are being made. In this example, he has selected three terms as subjects of word study: *Kecharitoméne* [full of grace]; *Dialogisomai* [discuss, explain]; *Paralambano* [personal relatives rather than married]. In each case, a word [Kecharitoméne] used solely once here and nowhere else in Scripture, or only once correctly by Mary [Dialogisomai], or once correctly by St. Joseph [Paralambano], helps us to understand a key, unique aspect of divine revelation conveyed to us by Mary. Once we know how to differentiate with Mary, between correct and incorrect meanings of these key words and the unique features of the proper usage, we find ourselves able to follow Mary and her associates in better grasping the implications of revealed teaching.

This reverent approach to Revelation does not detract from faith. On the contrary, faith is the very basis of study to attain the meaning of these mysteries. It helps us to realize the joy of studying theology, of discovering the links with one segment of Scripture and another.

What St. Maximilian Kolbe insists is so important in studying theology is to begin with a great devotion to Jesus and Mary. The more we situate our theology in this manner, the more we will find what St. Bonaventure calls the three modes making such theology possible: the symbolic mode or word study; the rational mode or study of ideas or lines of thought; the mystical mode or that mode of contemplating because we try to love God as much as Mary does.

And the more we do this, the more we will learn the whole of theology and why this is so in the words of Fr. Giacinto: *At the Incarnation the Divine Word became a creature; and the word of a creature became as though divine.* The Divine Word is Jesus; the word of this creature is none other than the word of the Mother of God and our Mother. Once we realize Mary's acceptance of the divine call to be Mother of Jesus, we begin to appreciate why our motherly Mediatrix is so good a teacher of theology, one "who kept all these things pondering them in her heart" (cf. *Lk* 2:19; 51) so that they might fill our hearts.

Fr. Peter Damian Fehlner

MARY AS MEDIATRIX IN LUMEN GENTIUM 62

In Continuity with Guadalupe, Fatima and St. Maximilian Kolbe

Gloria Falcão Dodd

Marian Symposium 2013
The Year of Faith, the New Evangelization, and Our Lady
Saturday, October 12, 2013, Shrine of Our Lady of
Guadalupe, La Crosse, Wisconsin

Introduction

Thank you for your kind introduction and your gracious welcome which is a good way to start a talk for the Year of Faith. As Bishop Fulton Sheen once said about applause, "At the start of a lecture, it is **a manifestation of faith**. In the middle, it is a sign of hope. At the end, it is always charity."[1] In keeping with the theme of the Year of Faith, it is appropriate to start with the Act of Faith presented in the *Compendium of the Catechism of the Catholic Church*:

> O my God, I firmly believe that you are one God in three divine Persons, Father, Son, and Holy Spirit. I believe that your divine Son became man and died for our sins and that he will come to judge the living and the dead. I believe these and all the truths which

---

[1] Joan Detz, *It's Not What You Say, It's How You Say It: Ready-To-Use Advice for Presentations, Speeches, and Other Speaking Occasions, Large and Small* (New York, NY: St. Martin's Press, 2000), 39.

the Holy Catholic Church teaches because you have revealed them who are eternal truth and wisdom, who can neither deceive nor be deceived. In this faith I intend to live and die. Amen.[2]

In this Year of Faith, why does this talk focus on *Lumen Gentium*? In his apostolic letter, *Porta Fidei*, or "*The Door of Faith*," Benedict XVI made October 12, 2012 – November 24, 2013, the Year of Faith to celebrate the 50th Anniversary of the Second Vatican Council and the 30th Anniversary of the *Catechism of the Catholic Church*.[3] Benedict XVI asked Catholics to know Christ better by studying the official documents of Vatican II and the *CCC*.[4] Why? Held from 1963–1965, Vatican II is the most recent ecumenical council of the pope and the bishops of the world. As Vatican II clarified in *Lumen Gentium* 25, the Holy Spirit infallibly protects from error these official teaching documents of all the bishops in union with the pope.[5] Of the 16 official documents that Vatican II published, only four were named Constitutions. Of these four Constitutions, two, *Dei Verbum* and *Lumen Gentium,* were the two "Dogmatic Constitutions," i.e., especially focused on the dogmas of the Church. Published in November of 1964, *Lumen Gentium, The Dogmatic Constitution on the Church,* had an entire chapter focused on Mary, and in that Chapter 8, section 62 validated the Church's use of the title "Mediatrix" for Mary. A year later *Dei Verbum, The Dogmatic Constitution on Divine Revelation*, provided a context that is needed for this topic.[6]

---

2   *Compendium of the Catechism of the Catholic Church* (Washington, D.C.: United States Conference of Catholic Bishops, 2006), 191.

3   Benedict XVI, *Porta Fidei*, n. 4, October 11, 2011. Vatican.va. http://www.vatican.va/holy_father/benedict_xvi/motu_proprio/documents/hf_ben-xvi_motu-proprio_20111011_porta-fidei_en.html.

4   *Porta Fidei*, n. 5 and 11.

5   *Lumen Gentium: The Dogmatic Constitution on the Church*, n. 25, in Austin Flannery, ed., *Vatican Council II: The Conciliar and Post Conciliar Documents*, rev. ed. (Collegeville, MN: Liturgical Press, 1984), n. 25. Henceforth, *Lumen Gentium* will be cited in the text, sometimes shortened as *LG*.

6   *Dei Verbum: The Dogmatic Constitution on Divine Revelation*, in Flannery, *Vatican Council II*. Henceforth, *Dei Verbum* will be cited in the text as *DV*.

In particular, *Dei Verbum* made an important distinction between public and private revelation. God's communication to man has shown forth in deeds and in words over the centuries, culminating in Christ, the fullness of The Truth (*DV* 1–4). Christ's one deposit of truth is then passed down from the Apostles to us today by Sacred Tradition, some of which is written down as the Sacred Scriptures (*DV* 7). While the truths called "dogmas"—taught by the Church as divinely revealed—do not change, the Holy Spirit guides the believers' reflection on the divinely revealed truths so that there is "a growth in the understanding of the realities and the words which have been handed down" (*DV* 8). Thus, the Church's doctrines, i.e., official teachings on matters of faith and morals, develop organically; as Bl. John Henry Newman explained in his famous *Essay on the Development of Christian Doctrine*: doctrines grow or expand to include logical deductions from the premises but never contradict the past.[7] The *Catechism of the Catholic Church* 65–67, while explaining this development, brings out both the explicit and implicit truths of revelation: "it remains for Christian faith gradually to grasp its full significance over the course of the centuries" (66).[8] With some of the recent media shock over papal statements, it is important to remember that dogmas and doctrines are both different from disciplines, i.e., the Church's instructions on how to follow or live out the doctrines; Church disciplines, such as priestly celibacy, can and have changed according to the cultures and times.[9] Such media confusion reinforces the importance of knowing the difference between Church dogmas and doctrines, that develop but do

---

[7] John Henry Newman, *Essay on the Development of Christian Doctrine* (London: B.M. Pickering, 1878), 73, 363.

[8] *Catechism of the Catholic Church*, 2nd edition, 1997, United States Conference of Catholic Bishops, http://www.usccb.org/beliefs-and-teachings/what-we-believe/catechism/catechism-of-the-catholic-church/epub/index.cfm. Henceforth, the *Catechism of the Catholic Church* will be cited in the text as *CCC*.

[9] F. Brinley Bruton, "Pope Francis' No. 2: Clerical celibacy is open to discussion," NBC news, Sep. 11, 2013, http://worldnews.nbcnews.com/_news/2013/09/11/20433950-pope-francis-no-2-clerical-celibacy-is-open-to-discussion?lite.

not contradict the past, and Church disciplines, that indeed can change in time and places.

Although *Dei Verbum* does not address private revelations, i.e., visions or locutions made to mystics, the *CCC* 67 clarifies this point. Even those private revelations that are approved by the Church "do not belong, however, to the deposit of faith. It is not their role to improve or complete Christ's definitive Revelation, but to help live more fully by it in a certain period of history." Thus, approved Marian apparitions show us how to apply the Church's teachings.

Therefore, today, this paper will try to show that Mary's universal mediation has been taught by *Lumen Gentium* in continuity with the past examples of two famous Marian apparitions and in continuity with St. Maximilian Kolbe's teaching, and that Mary's universal mediation remains the model for the New Evangelization today. Therefore, this paper will first define what Mary's universal mediation of grace means before proceeding to review Mary's actions and words in her apparitions as Our Lady of Guadalupe and then Our Lady of Fatima. This paper will then present highlights of St. Maximilian Kolbe's teachings, and of *Lumen Gentium*, Chapter 8. For the sake of simplicity, only one example of each point will be provided, although many more could be found. The paper will conclude by fusing the helpful ideas from Mary's apparitions and the teachings as a guide to a fruitful apostolate in the New Evangelization.

A Definition of Terms – Mary, Mediatrix of All Graces

First, to explain that Mary has a universal mediation of grace, a definition of terms is necessary. St. Thomas Aquinas defined a mediator as a *mean* or middle person who is simultaneously different from and similar to two extremes and that unites the two extremes. "Mediatrix" is the feminine form of the Latin term. In the hypostatic union, Christ is the one and only mediator who is a perfect and permanent union of God and man, having one divine person and two natures: human and divine, and whose Death on the Cross reunited the forgiven humanity with God. However, others participate in mediation in a subordinate and dependent way in Christ's primary and independent mediation, such as prophets who prepare people to be united with God, and ministers who sacramentally unite people with God.[10] Thus, Mary participates in Christ's mediation in a subordinate, dependent, and yet true mediation between God and man; first, for her role in the Incarnation, and then for her role in uniting Christ with man.

For a definition of "grace," the glossary of the *CCC* provides its theological meaning in general as "the free and undeserved gift from God that gives us the ability to respond to our vocation to become his adopted children." The *Catechism* then specifies different types of grace. Sanctifying grace is a share in God's "divine life and friendship with us in an habitual gift, a stable and supernatural disposition that enables the soul to live with God, to act by his love." Actual grace is God's "help to conform our lives to his will. Sacramental grace and special graces (charisms, the grace of one's state of life) are gifts of the Holy Spirit to help us live out our Christian vocation." This paper will refer more to grace in the sense of freely-given participation in God's life, i.e., spiritual life, while the other meanings of grace are not excluded because this paper aims to show that Mary mediates all grace, or all graces, depending on which sense of the word one uses.

How can Mary mediate all grace or all graces? She was united with Christ, subordinately and dependently, but still truly, in the redemption of all people. Her union with Christ was preceded by her union with the Holy Spirit who had dwelt in her from her Immaculate Conception and onward. The Holy Spirit formed Christ's body in her womb; and God's ways do not change. The Holy Spirit continues to form the Mystical Body of Christ in her spiritual womb. Thus, every grace we receive from Christ with the Holy Spirit comes to us through Mary.

Our Lady of Guadalupe's Mediation

At this lovely Shrine of Our Lady of Guadalupe, it is only fitting that this presentation starts with Our Lady of Guadalupe's

---

[10] Thomas Aquinas, *Summa Theologica* III (Westminster, MD: Christian Classics, 1981), Q. 26, a. 1 & 2, and III Supplement, Q. 90, a. 2, c.

mediation; it is also chronologically the first of the events to be studied. And as the saying goes, "actions speak louder than words."[11] Therefore, Mary's deeds in her apparitions of December 9–12, 1531, to St. Juan Diego, are even more powerful than her words.

How did Mary act as a universal Mediatrix at this apparition? Five actions stand out:

> OUTREACHING – First, as a saint in heaven, Mary reached out to Juan Diego on earth, calling him by name when he came to Tepeyac Hill. He had not asked for her to appear. She came on her own initiative, or more precisely, prompted by the Holy Spirit, she came. And in the last apparition when Juan Diego was trying to avoid her, she even came down the hill and blocked his passage![12]

> QUESTIONING – Mary's style was dialogic. In her first and last apparitions, she asked Juan Diego where he was going, inviting a response. Other times she asked rhetorical questions just to reassure Juan Diego, e.g., "Am I not here, I, who am your Mother?"[13]

> PREGNANT – Mary's rather substantial waist and her black belt tied so high indicated in an Aztec culture, that she was pregnant at the time of the apparition.[14] But Jesus Christ had already been born! Who was in her womb? The Mystical Body of Christ is still being formed spiritually in her womb (*Rev* 12:17).

---

11 Bartlett Jere Whiting, *Early American Proverbs and Proverbial Phrases* (Cambridge, MA.: Belknap Press of Harvard University Press, 1977), 3.

12 *A Handbook on Guadalupe* (New Bedford, MA: Franciscan Friars of the Immaculate, 2001), 200.

13 *Handbook on Guadalupe*, 194, 200.

14 Janet Barber, "Holy Mary of Guadalupe, Prolife Patron," in *Handbook on Guadalupe*, 135.

Subordinate to the Church's authority – She respected the authority of the bishop for the well-being of his diocese. She did not have a church built without his permission.[15]

Miraculous image – Mary left a sacramental that then disposed nine million native people to convert in twelve years after the apparition. She chose to mediate through an image that prompted the people to recognize that she was one of them.[16]

Thus, Mary's deeds show a spirit of love, solidarity and subsidiarity in her actions at Guadalupe.

Mary's words at Guadalupe further refine an understanding of her mediation. For the sake of brevity, this paper will provide only one example for each category below:

Maternal/universal – Her comforting words are a treasure: "I am truly your merciful Mother, yours and all the people who live united in this land and of all the other people of different ancestries…."[17] Her motherhood is not limited to Juan Diego, the Aztecs, and the Spanish, but includes all people of all races and all times! This universal motherhood is the foundation for her mediation.

Magnifying the Lord – Mary's mediation has the glory of God as her ultimate purpose. Why does she ask for a church to be built? As she herself said, "A little house built here for me, in which I will show Him, I will exalt Him and make Him manifest."[18]

Inclusive/delegating – When Juan Diego begged Our Lady to send someone more important to be the messenger after he had failed in his first attempt to convince Bishop Zumárraga, Our Lady replied that "I do not lack servants and

---

[15] *Handbook on Guadalupe*, 194.

[16] Warren Carroll, *Our Lady of Guadalupe and the Conquest of Darkness* (Front Royal, VA: Christendom Publications, 1983), 17.

[17] *Handbook on Guadalupe*, 194.

[18] *Handbook on Guadalupe*, 194.

messengers to whom I can give the task of carrying out my words, who will carry out my will. But it is very necessary that **you** plead my cause and, **with your help, and through your mediation**, that my will be fulfilled" (emphasis added).[19] Thus, Mary's mediation deliberately included Juan Diego and the Bishop. She could have appeared directly to the Bishop if she had wanted to, but instead she chose Juan Diego to take her message to the Bishop. She could have had the angels build a church without any human help, but she chose to involve the Bishop and all those who then donated and worked on the building. Just as God has been delegating to her and allowing her the joy of cooperating with him in his work, Mary delegates to her children to share her joy in doing God's work.

BRINGING CHRIST TO MAN – Again she says, "I will give Him to the people in all my personal love, in my compassion, in my help, in my protection."[20]

UNIVERSAL HEALER – "Here I … will heal all their sorrows, their hardships and sufferings."[21] In this sense, universality refers to her ability to intercede for the healing of any cross.

Thus, Mary's speech to Juan Diego illustrates clearly how Mary's humble motherhood glorifies God, and unites all people to Christ. Our Lady of Guadalupe is a wonderful example of how Mary is the Mediatrix to the Mediator. Along with her evangelization of the native peoples, she had already begun a form of New Evangelization, i.e., calling the Spanish conquistadors who had lapsed, to return to a practice of their Christian faith, especially to the understanding of the human dignity of the native peoples who are their brothers and sisters, with Mary as their common mother.

Our Lady of Fatima's Mediation

The next example of mediation is Our Lady's appearances to the three children of Fatima—Lucia dos Santos, Francisco and Jacinta

---

19 *Handbook on Guadalupe*, 197.

20 *Handbook on Guadalupe*, 194.

21 *Handbook on Guadalupe*, 194.

Marto. In the series of apparitions that started on May 13th and officially ended on October 13, 1917, Our Lady's message was given in a post-Enlightenment context with many lapsed Catholics who had become agnostics and even atheists in Portugal, particularly in the face of WWI's terrible toll of death. Thus, Mary's message, directed to Catholics in general, was already a New Evangelization calling lax and former Catholics to a fervent practice of their Faith. At Fatima, Our Lady's mediation takes some of the same actions as in her appearances at Guadalupe:

OUTREACHING – She initiated contact (May 13th).[22] The three children had not asked for her to appear.

INCLUSIVE/DELEGATING – She did not appear directly to the pastor, the bishop, or the pope, but rather had the three children take her message to them as well as to all the Church.[23]

DELIBERATE – She had clearly planned ahead because at the very first apparition she asked them to come for five more months. At the July 13th apparition, in response to Lucia's request, Mary promised a miracle in October.[24] She did advance planning, with promotions starting three months in advance!

PUBLIC SIGNS – By the second apparition, other people besides the three children were experiencing supernatural phenomena. Even in August when the children had been kidnapped and were not even present, some saw a cloud come down on the holm oak; others felt a change in temperature, or heard sounds like the buzzing of a bee.[25] The grand finale was the miracle of the sun, on October 13th, with its spinning, show of colors, and the immediate drying of the ground experienced by all

---

[22] Robert J. Fox, Antonio Maria Martins, and Maria Lucia Irmal, *Documents on Fatima and the Memoirs of Sister Lucia*, (Waite Park, MN: Fatima Family Apostolate, 2002), 310.

[23] The request for daily Rosaries was made at all of the six Fatima apparitions in 1917, but it was not until 1929 that Sr. Lucia was told to give a message to the pope, *Documents*, 11, 283–284, 378.

[24] *Documents*, 152–153. John de Marchi, *Fatima the Facts*, trans. I.M. Kingsbury (Cork, Ireland: Mercier, 1950), 65.

[25] *Documents*, 159–160. Marchi, 54.

present—thousands of devout believers, as well as atheists and agnostics.[26]

CENTRALITY OF CHRIST – In the midst of that miracle of the sun, one of the scenes that the three children saw was Christ in the center of the sun, in between Joseph and Mary (October 13th).[27]

Mary's public and private messages at Fatima illustrate additional qualities of her mediation:

INSTRUCTIVE – By publicly asking everyone to pray the daily Rosary with its fifty Hail Marys, Mary taught us the value and power of her intercessory role, even stating: "Continue to say the Rosary every day in honor of Our Lady of the Rosary to obtain the peace of the world and the end of the war, because **only I can obtain it**" (July 13th, emphasis added).[28] By privately requesting that Russia be consecrated to her Immaculate Heart, Mary again taught how God chose to work through her in bringing the gift of conversion (July 13th).[29] Mary's prophetic words are a type of dispositive mediation to prepare people to receive God's grace.

EMPOWERING – In a statement probably dear to many a teacher, Mary told Lucia she must learn to read (June 13th).[30] Her command prepared Lucia to be able to convey the messages that would help people to cooperate with the graces from God.

BRINGING MAN TO JESUS – The prayer Mary taught the children to offer sacrifices is addressed to Jesus, not herself: "O Jesus, this is for love of Thee, for the conversion of sinners, and in reparation for the sins committed against the Immaculate Heart of Mary" (July 13th).[31]

---

26 *Documents*, 197–201, 205–209, 211, etc. Marchi, 135.

27 *Documents*, 190, 194, 196.

28 Marchi, 65. Similar translation in *Documents*, 153.

29 Marchi, 79.

30 *Documents*, 152. Marchi, 67.

31 Marchi, 66.

Subordinate to Church authority – Her request was made to the pope and the bishops asking them to consecrate the world to her Immaculate Heart.[32]

Promotional – When Lucia asked for a miracle so that people would believe, Mary promised a public miracle three months in advance. She certainly knows how to draw a crowd!

Thus, in both actions and words, Our Lady of Fatima exemplified a subordinate mediation that drew man to Christ and those in the Church into a mediation subordinate to her own. These public appearances concluded on October 13, 1917, just four days before St. Maximilian Kolbe founded his Marian apostolate.

St. Maximilian Kolbe on Marian Mediation

At this Shrine tended so kindly by the Franciscan Friars of the Immaculate, one must be sure to include St. Maximilian Kolbe. And as a well-integrated person, Kolbe's actions complemented his words. He asked of others only what he himself did first. And what did he do about Mary's mediation?

Marian consecration – Having experienced his own Marian apparition that prompted him as a boy to choose the two crowns of purity and martyrdom, it was no surprise that as a sixteen year old seminarian, he consecrated himself to Mary.[33] This entrustment was renewed in 1917 when he started the Militia Immaculatae.[34]

Militia of the Immaculata – This group was Kolbe's deliberate participation in Mary's mission of crushing the head of the serpent (*Gen* 3:15). On October 17, 1917, he founded it with six other seminarians in Rome. He chose to succeed

---

[32] *Documents*, 395–386, Sr. Lucia's letter of December 2, 1940, to Pope Pius XII recounts how Our Lady asked for this in 1917 but it remained a secret until 1926 and then publicly announced by the Bishop of Leiria in 1939. Marchi, 66–67.

[33] Peter Damian Fehlner, "Is the Martyr of Charity a Heretic?," 97–103, in Francis M. Kalvelage, ed., *Kolbe: Saint of the Immaculata* (New Bedford, MA: Franciscans of the Immaculate, 2001), 17, 21.

[34] *Kolbe*, 34.

in the spiritual battle by working under the subordinate mediation of the Immaculate Virgin Mary.[35]

MIRACULOUS MEDAL – Kolbe made great use of the Miraculous Medal, or the medal of the Immaculate Conception, as it was formally named. He wore it and prayed its invocation. He then made wearing it, saying its prayer, and also distributing it, requirements for membership in the Militia Immaculatae. He was an inspiring model in showing its effectiveness in bringing about conversions.[36]

With the conviction that came from these lived experiences of the power of Mary's mediation, Kolbe taught often and explicitly about Mary's universal mediation in many talks and writings. Here are just a few highlights:

UNITED WITH THE HOLY SPIRIT – The basis for Mary's mediation from Kolbe's perspective is the most intimate and close relationship possible for a human being to have with the Holy Spirit. She was completely filled with the Holy Spirit and so united to him that he works through her.[37] But the difficulty is how to express this relationship? A typically Franciscan approach would be to call Mary the Spouse of the Holy Spirit, as Kolbe did.[38]

But Kolbe's original contributions were to propose new descriptions of Mary as the "created Immaculate Conception," and "the personification of the Holy Spirit," who is the uncreated Immaculate Conception, i.e., the fruit of the love

---

[35] *Kolbe*, 34–5, 37.

[36] *Kolbe*, 35, 37, 41–42. St. Maximilian Kolbe, "The Ideals and Program of The Knights of the Immaculata: (International Latin name: Militia Immaculatae or "MI") in the words of its Founder: A brochure for distribution among priests by Niepokalanow in 1938." Trans, Bernard Geiger. Consecration: Militia of the Immaculate. http://www.consecration.com/default.aspx?id=33, accessed September 11, 2013.

[37] Rosella Bignami, "Fr. Luigi Faccenda, O.F.M., Conv., and the Kolbean Marian and Missionary Charism," *Marian Studies* 54 (2003): 149.

[38] Peter Damian Fehlner, "Is the Martyr of Charity a Heretic?" in *Kolbe: Saint of the Immaculate*, edited by Francis M. Kalvelage (New Bedford, MA: Franciscans of the Immaculate, 2001), 102.

between the Father and the Son.[39] Kolbe's most controversial description of Mary was as a quasi-incarnation of the Holy Spirit, although there is really no need for confusion because Kolbe clearly distinguished quasi or almost an incarnation, from Christ's Incarnation, where in a hypostatic union there was only one divine person, with two natures—human and divine. Kolbe also clearly distinguished Mary as a human person with a human nature from the divine person of the Holy Spirit.[40] As Kolbe himself wrote, "It is an unexplainable but perfect union by reason of which the Holy Spirit does not act except through the Immaculata, his Spouse. She, therefore, is the Mediatrix of all the graces of the Most Holy Spirit."[41]

EMPOWERING THE APOSTOLATE – Kolbe understood that Mary, as the Mediatrix of all graces, empowers the apostolate. In a recruiting leaflet for the Militia Immaculata, Kolbe described Mary's mediation as the prompt, the shield, and the source of success for the apostolic worker; therefore he required this consecration to "give ourselves to the Immaculate Virgin as instruments in her immaculate hands."[42]

BRINGING MAN TO CHRIST – Kolbe saw Mary's mediation as a path to Christ, neither detracting nor diverting from Christ's

---

[39] Ernesto Piacenti, *Panorama of the Marian Doctrine of Bl. Maximilian Kolbe*, Trans. Donald Kos (Kenosha, WI: Franciscan Marytown Press, 1975), 32–33; Grzegorz M. Bartosik, "Rapporto fra lo Spirito Santo e Maria come principio della mediazione mariana negli ultimi scritti (1935–1941) di San Massimiliano Maria Kolbe," *Miles Immaculatae* 27 (1991): 245, emphasized the originality of Kolbe's idea.

[40] Piacenti, *Panorama*, 32–33.

[41] Piacenti, *Panorama*, p. 33, citing Kolbe's Letter 28/7/1935. Similar expressions are found in: Conference 25/9/1937; Conference 28/6/1936. Bartosik, "Rapporto," pp. 263–265, noted that Kolbe certainly held and taught Mary's universal mediation of grace with at least 20 written references, sometimes using the title, "Mediatrix of All Graces." Giuseppe Simbula, "Lo Spirito Santo nell'esperienza spirituale e nella riflessione teologica di S. Massimiliano Kolbe." *Miles Immaculatae* 33 (1997): 472, thought that Kolbe's use of "Mediatrix of All Grace" was more of a pious expression than a careful theological statement since she couldn't have mediated her own first grace.

[42] Kolbe, "The Ideals and Program of The Knights of the Immaculata." Bartosik, "Rapporto," 251, noted this entrustment is similar to St. Louis Marie de Montfort's consecration, but with Kolbe's special emphasis on Mary's Immaculate Conception. Bignami, 146.

one mediation (*1 Tim* 2:5). "We know perfectly well that the object of all devotion is God. In the same way, the cult offered to the Immaculata is a direct means to this end. We should search for Jesus through her and not in another place but in her. We pass with her to the other."[43]

Thus, St. Maximilian Kolbe lived and taught the mystery of Mary's Immaculate mediation. Kolbe affirmed the Church's teaching of Mary as the Mediatrix of All Graces and suggested new ways to explain it. With his death in 1941, Kolbe did not live to see the Second Vatican Council's teaching on Mary's mediation, but his work was in harmony with it.

Lumen Gentium on Mary's mediation

At the Second Vatican Council, there had been much dispute about Mary's title as "Mediatrix of all graces." With Christ as the starting point, some theologians had emphasized Mary as the closest to Christ, the One Mediator of *1 Timothy* 2:5, and therefore, in a "Christo-typical" approach affirmed Mary's universal mediation. Other theologians opposed this Marian title, because they focused on Mary's relationship with the Church, or they could not explain how Mary could mediate all graces. Others worried that such a title would be contrary to the pastoral and ecumenical purposes of the Council. These "ecclesio-typical" theologians persuaded the Council Fathers to include the Marian doctrines within the *Constitution on the Church*, that came to be known as *Lumen Gentium*, specifically in Chapter 8. These theologians also succeeded in eliminating the specification "of all graces" in the compromise statement of *Lumen Gentium,* n. 62: "the Blessed Virgin is invoked in the Church under the titles of Advocate, Helper, Benefactress, and Mediatrix."[44] The press and some theologians misconstrued the omission of the extended title as a rejection of the Church's past

---

[43] Piacenti, *Panorama*, 37, citing Conference 25/4/1937.

[44] Gloria Falcão Dodd, *The Virgin Mary, Mediatrix of All Grace: History and Theology of the Movement for a Dogmatic Definition from 1896 to 1964* (New Bedford, MA: Academy of the Immaculate, 2012), 269–293.

teaching and a downgrading of Mary.[45] But was this an accurate assessment? Perhaps not! A comparison of what *Lumen Gentium* stated with the earlier definition of Mary's universal mediation will provide a better answer.

As the Council intended, *Lumen Gentium* took a pastoral and ecumenical approach that started with a gentle indication that Mary is invoked as a Mediatrix. But if the Church invokes Mary as a Mediatrix, the Church does so because Mary is a Mediatrix! *Lumen Gentium* also goes on to clearly present Mary as:

UNITING GOD AND MAN IN CHRIST – She was named as the "Mother of God," n. 52–53 (more in n. 55–56: "Mother of the Redeemer," n. 55, "Mother of Jesus," n. 56).

BRINGING CHRIST TO MAN, AND MAN TO CHRIST – Section 60 stated that Mary's "salutary influence on men ... does not hinder in any way the immediate union of the faithful with Christ but on the contrary fosters it" (n. 60).

SUBORDINATE TO AND DEPENDENT ON CHRIST, THE ONE MEDIATOR – *Lumen Gentium* clearly stated "... Mary's function as mother of men in no way obscures or diminishes this unique mediation on Christ, but rather shows its power. ... It flows forth from the superabundance of the merits of Christ, rests on His mediation, depends entirely on it and draws all its power from it" (n. 60).

Thus, *Lumen Gentium* validated the Church's application of "Mediatrix" to Mary because she certainly fulfilled the general definition and role of a Mediatrix between God and man, as well as between Christ and man.

But did *Lumen Gentium* concede to her a mediation of grace? *Lumen Gentium* did agree on the interpretation of grace as **spiritual life** stating: "in a wholly singular way she cooperated by her obedience, faith and burning charity in the work of the Savior in *restoring supernatural life in souls*. And for this reason she is *a*

---

[45] William G. Most, *Our Lady in Doctrine and Devotion* (Alexandria, VA: Notre Dame Institute Press, 1995), http://www.ewtn.com/library/THEOLOGY/MARY523.HTM, described the post-Vatican II confusion about Mary.

mother to us in the order of grace." (n. 61, emphasis added). This statement provided a solid premise that, combined with the second step that motherhood is indeed a type of mediation, yields the conclusion that Mary is a Mediatrix of grace.

In regards to the universality of Mary's mediation, *Lumen Gentium* confirmed the concept but expressed it in other words; the ecclesio-typical approach noted that Mary is "a type of the Church in ... *perfect union with Christ*" (n. 63, emphasis added). Carlo Balic, one of the two primary co-authors of Chapter 8 of *Lumen Gentium* had explained that the footnotes help to interpret the document.[46] Applying this helpful principle, footnote 16 cited Pius XII's radio message to Fatima on May 13, 1946, in which the pope explained that Mary's permanent association with Christ "in the distribution of *the graces which flow from the Redemption*" (emphasis added).[47] Thinking logically about this statement, which graces come from Christ's redemption? All graces! Footnote 16 also helped to answer this question by citing *Adjutricem populi*, an encyclical by Leo XIII, who described Mary as "the Dispenser of *all heavenly gifts*" (emphasis added).[48]

The last part of the earlier definition of Mary's universal mediation had described it in terms of her union with the Holy Spirit in forming the members of the Mystical Body of Christ. *Lumen Gentium* progressed to incorporate this idea, although this may be one of the weaker parts of the document. *Lumen Gentium* said very simply that Mary is "the temple of the Holy Spirit" (n. 53), but also explained that she is the "Mother of the members of Christ," (n. 53) which is a stronger statement of her mediation (see also n. 54 – "mother of men").

Therefore, *Lumen Gentium* taught explicitly that Mary can be called a Mediatrix and mother of grace, and implied that this was to be understood in the sense of a universal mediation. There was

---

[46] This principle of interpretation was given by Carlo Balić, "*El Capitulo VIII de la Constitucion 'Lumen Gentium' comparado con el Primer Esquema de la B. Virgen Madre de la Iglesia,*" *Estudios Marianos* 27 (1966):166, and William G. Most, *Vatican II: Marian Council* (Athlone, Ireland: Alba House, 1972), 33.

[47] Dodd, 290–291.

[48] Leo XIII's *Adjutricem populi* (September 5, 1895, *ASS* 28 (1895–1896): 130.

a true development that went beyond what had been said officially about Mary's mediation in any previous Council document. Although it did not directly affirm the title of Mary as Mediatrix of All Grace, *Lumen Gentium* remained open to further organic development. As n. 54 expressed it, *Lumen Gentium* was: "… not a complete doctrine on Mary, nor to decide those questions which the work of theologians has not yet fully clarified. Those opinions therefore may be lawfully retained which are propounded in Catholic schools concerning her, who occupies a place in the Church which is the highest after Christ and also closest to us" (n. 54).

Having completed this review of the apparitions and doctrines culminating with the developments of the Second Vatican Council, some applications of this beautiful doctrine to the New Evangelization can be proposed.

Mediating with Mary in the New Evangelization

Since Mary is the model of the Church, the Church should learn how to engage in the New Evangelization "in the School of Mary," as Pope John Paul II expressed it.[49] Synthesizing some general ideas from all that has been said about these apparitions and doctrines, three points remained as constants either explicitly or implicitly for an imitation of Mary's qualities:

> CONSECRATION TO MARY – Those apostles who belong to Mary as her child, her messenger and her soldier, place themselves under her protection. Mary transforms those who are consecrated to her so that she "turns their weakness into strength," making them effective mediators, subordinate to her mediation, and together with Mary, subordinate to Christ's mediation.[50]

---

[49] John Paul II, *Rosarium Virginis*, October 16, 2002, n. 1. Vatican. http://www.vatican.va/holy_father/john_paul_ii/apost_letters/documents/hf_jp-ii_apl_20021016_rosarium-virginis-mariae_en.html

[50] Part of the Promise in *The Official Handbook of the Legion of Mary* (Dublin: Concilium Legionis Mariae, 2005), 91.

MATERNAL / LOVING – The apostle who is dedicated to Mary is mindful of acting as Mary–to see as Mary does and to serve Christ in others.[51]

SUBORDINATE TO CHURCH AUTHORITY – Obedience to the pope, one's bishop, and one's pastor brings the necessary graces from God. Ask permission from the proper ecclesiastical authorities before attempting some apostolic work. And if they say "no," when the Marian apostle is convinced that what he is asking is God's will, then this consecrated person can ask them what proof they might need in order to say "yes." If they still say "no," then the apostle will wait patiently to ask their successor, or another bishop or pastor.

Both apparitions illustrated how Mary's actions provided an example worthy of imitation:

REACH OUT – *Initiate conversations.* Evangelizing requires the willingness to speak first to people whom one does not know, and even chasing after someone who might be trying to avoid the apostle. Welcome the visitor at church by chatting after Mass. Invite one's new neighbor or one's lapsed Catholic family member to come with you to church; it helps if there are coffee and donuts afterwards, too!

ASK QUESTIONS – *Dialogue.* Mary asked Juan Diego, "Where are you going?" This is a profound question to ask anyone about their life and their afterlife. Another gentle question to a lapsed Catholic could be: "Have you ever considered coming back to the Catholic Church?" If they say "no," "Why not?" is a good follow-up. Learning someone's objections is the first step in overcoming them.

PLAN EVENTS AND ADVERTISE – *Tell others about events at least three months in advance.* Marketing and media can be used to promote the Catholic Faith as EWTN, Radio Maria, and Air Maria have already shown.

---

[51] "Standing instructions," of the Legion of Mary, *Official Handbook*, 109.

Include/delegate – *Invite others to share in the apostolate.* The New Evangelization requires the organization of people to work together with Mary and with each other to accomplish more than anyone could do alone. The wise and humble apostle learns from those who are more experienced; the learned and experienced would be wise to train others to take their place.

Imitating Our Lady of Guadalupe provides ideas for some specific techniques:

Show her image – She gave this visual and scientifically-verified miracle that appeals to a modern world. In recent years, Mary's image on the tilma has been even more clearly understood to be an on-going miracle by its very existence for more than the twenty years that the cactus fibers would normally last, and the image survived a bomb blast on November 14, 1921.[52] Scientific testing has shown that the image was not painted, was not a photograph, but instead seems to float on the surface of the tilma.[53] Discovered in 1929 and publicized in 1951, the reflection of nine people can be seen three times in Our Lady's eyes—right side up on the cornea's exterior, the back of the lens, and then upside down on the front of the lens—just as a human eye sees things![54] These documented facts can be used to reach out to the scientifically-minded modern person.

Prolife work – Protect life in a culture of death. Our Lady of Guadalupe appeared as a pregnant mother to the native peoples of Mexico where the Aztec culture had indeed been a culture of death; by law, 1,000 human victims had to be sacrificed every year on every temple in the Aztec empire, with at least 50,000 victims annually.[55] Mary came to bring the Gospel of Life that overcomes the Culture of Death similar

---

[52] Francis Johnston, *The Wonder of Guadalupe: The Origin and Cult of the Miraculous Image of the Blessed Virgin in Mexico.* (Rockford, IL: Tan Books, 1981), 117–119.

[53] *Handbook on Guadalupe*, 61.

[54] *Handbook on Guadalupe*, 89–91.

[55] Carroll, 8.

to today with over 2,000 children aborted daily in the United States alone.[56] Human life is disrespected worldwide with wars, contraception, abortion, sterilization, and the death penalty.[57] Many lapsed Catholics are going in for abortions; there are rosaries hanging on their cars in the parking lot. Many former Catholics are active in the prolife movement but left the Catholic Church; some say "I never heard a priest or others in the church speak about the pro-life movement." How important it is that we prevent people from leaving, and reach out to bring the lapsed back!

Our Lady of Fatima also models for us how to mediate in the New Evangelization by gathering people together in a rally and also having processions as they do at Fatima. A public spectacle brings people! A Rosary for peace in today's terrorist culture and fears of another world war very much touches the heart of both practicing and lapsed Catholics to pray together for world peace. World Youth Days show how a rally is a wonderful opportunity for a short instruction; and when combined with benediction, it is a wonderful way to focus on the centrality of Christ.

As an innocent victim who gave his life for another in a death camp, Koble exemplified a Marian response to a culture of death. Koble emphasized the importance of Marian consecration. Apostles need to live in, with and for Mary Immaculate to mediate under Mary's mediation. This consecrated union with Mary Immaculate requires one to be in the state of grace. Frequent confession helps apostles to maintain or to regain as much of a sinless state as possible.

Then the Miraculous Medal is a tangible expression of this consecration. This sacramental, especially when worn around the

---

[56] John Paul II, *Evangelium Vitae*, March 25, 1995, section 12, 19, 21, 24, 26, 28, 50, 64, 87, 95, and 100, described the "culture of death." Vatican. http://www.vatican.va/holy_father/john_paul_ii/encyclicals/documents/hf_jp-ii_enc_25031995_evangelium-vitae_en.html. "Fact Sheet: Induced Abortion in the United States," The Guttmacher Institute, http://www.guttmacher.org/pubs/fb_induced_abortion.html, "In 2011, 1.06 million abortions were performed...." Divided by 365 days in a year, that would mean 2,904 babies killed per day.

[57] *Evangelium Vitae*, 13, 17, 27, etc.

neck, and with recitation of the daily prayer, is a powerful way to be open to the graces that God wishes to give to apostles through the one conceived without sin, and then, through the forgiven apostles, to the world. Each one can become "a living Miraculous Medal"![58] These evangelizers can gives these medals to lapsed Catholics and expect great things; these medals came to be called "miraculous" for very good reasons. Thus, Kolbe reminded us that the spiritual state of the apostles affects their ability to mediate, and that Mary is the mold that forms effective apostles in the New Evangelization.

Lumen Gentium can play a role in the New Evangelization as well. It can be a little intimidating as an official Church document. But study groups can help. First, however, each person needs to have a copy of *Lumen Gentium* and it is easy enough today to get one. Anyone can download an electronic version from the Vatican website. However, a physical copy could be more useful for highlighting, making notes in the margin, and then keeping it. While it helps to have someone like a priest, deacon, religious or maybe a religion teacher to lead a study group, there are many study guides available for free on the Internet.

Lumen Gentium also models a style of proclaiming Mary in the context of Christ and the Church. Mary's mediation flows precisely from her maternal mediation with Christ and with us, the body of Christ, the Church. Everyone has a mother! And the analogy of an unborn child in his mother's womb is an easy way for many people to understand how Mary mediates everything for her unborn mystical body of Christ.

If someone is having trouble with the Title, "Mediatrix of All Graces," go back to the foundations. Focus on the main ideas. Explain the reasons for her mediation and then hopefully people can make that logical deduction to the truthful conclusion. Avoid disputes. Even if someone still disagrees with Mary's universal mediation of grace, friendly discussions, not arguments, win hearts.

---

[58] *Handbook of the Legion of Mary*, p. 345.

Conclusion

Hopefully this paper has shown what Mary's universal mediation means and how the apparitions of Our Lady of Guadalupe and Our Lady of Fatima illustrated some of the ways that Mary has mediated in specific times and places. St. Maximilian Kolbe's teaching provided deep insights into Mary's sinless mediation that is closely united to the action of the Holy Spirit. The text and even the footnotes of *Lumen Gentium* have helped the entire Church to understand more clearly the bases for Mary's maternal mediation in the order of grace, while remaining open to the Holy Spirit's next steps in the development of this doctrine. These apparitions and doctrines have suggested practical ways for Catholics to become consecrated apostles in the New Evangelization, distributing images of Our Lady of Guadalupe and Miraculous Medals to lapsed Catholics, engaging in prolife work and bringing people to rallies and candlelight processions. Knowing that the Church's mediation is dependent on Mary's, it is appropriate to close this paper with a prayer to Our Lady as Mediatrix of All Graces as the Immaculate Mediatrix in order to set all hearts on fire, in union with Her Immaculate Heart, to turn ever more to the Sacred Heart of Jesus:

> O Lord Jesus Christ, our mediator with the Father, Who has been pleased to appoint the Most Blessed Virgin, Your mother, to be our mother also, and our mediatrix with You, mercifully grant that whoever comes to You seeking Your favours may rejoice to receive all of them through her. Amen.

Mary Immaculate, Mediatrix of All Graces, pray for us.[59]

---

[59] Catena prayer in the *Official Handbook of the Legion of Mary*, 133.

BIBLIOGRAPHY

Aquinas, Thomas. *Summa Theologica*. Westminster, MD: Christian Classics, 1981.

Balić, Carlo. "*El Capitulo VIII de la Constitucion 'Lumen Gentium' comparado con el Primer Esquema de la B. Virgen Madre de la Iglesia,*" Estudios Marianos 27 (1966): 135–183.

Whiting, Jere Bartlett. *Early American Proverbs and Proverbial Phrases*. Cambridge, MA: Belknap Press of Harvard University Press, 1977.

Benedict XVI, *Porta Fidei*, n. 4, October 11, 2011. Vatican.va. http://www.vatican.va/holy_father/benedict_xvi/motu_proprio/documents/hf_ben-xvi_motu-proprio_20111011_porta-fidei_en.html.

Bruton, F. Brinley. "Pope Francis' No. 2: Clerical celibacy is open to discussion," NBC news, Sep. 11, 2013, http://worldnews.nbcnews.com/_news/2013/09/11/20433950-pope-francis-no-2-clerical-celibacy-is-open-to-discussion?lite.

Catechism of the Catholic Church, 2nd edition, 1997. United States Conference of Catholic Bishops. http://www.usccb.org/beliefs-and-teachings/what-we-believe/catechism/catechism-of-the-catholic-church/epub/index.cfm

Compendium of the Catechism of the Catholic Church. Washington, D.C.: United States Conference of Catholic Bishops, 2006.

Detz, Joan. *It's Not What You Say, It's How You Say It: Ready-To-Use Advice for Presentations, Speeches, and Other Speaking Occasions, Large and Small*. New York, NY: St. Martin's Press, 2000.

Dodd, Gloria Falcão. *The Virgin Mary, Mediatrix of All Grace: History and Theology of the Movement for a Dogmatic*

Definition from 1896 to 1964. New Bedford, MA: Academy of the Immaculate, 2012.

"Fact Sheet: Induced Abortion in the United States," The Guttmacher Institute, http://www.guttmacher.org/pubs/fb_induced_abortion.html.

Flannery, Austin, ed., *Vatican Council II: The Conciliar and Post Conciliar Documents*, rev. ed. Collegeville, MN: Liturgical Press, 1984.

John Paul II, *Evangelium Vitae*, March 25, 1995, Vatican. http://www.vatican.va/holy_father/john_paul_ii/encyclicals/documents/hf_jp-ii_enc_25031995_evangelium-vitae_en.html.

———. *Rosarium Virginis*, October 16, 2002, n. 1. Vatican. http://www.vatican.va/holy_father/john_paul_ii/apost_letters/documents/hf_jp-ii_apl_20021016_rosarium-virginis-mariae_en.html.

Leo XIII, *Adjutricem populi* (September 5, 1895, *ASS* 28 (1895–1896): 129–136.

Most, William G. *Our Lady in Doctrine and Devotion.* Alexandria, VA: Notre Dame Institute Press, 1995. http://www.ewtn.com/library/THEOLOGY/MARY523.HTM.

———. *Vatican II: Marian Council* (Athlone, Ireland: Alba House, 1972).

Newman, John Henry. *Essay on the Development of Christian Doctrine.* London: B.M. Pickering, 1878.

The Official Handbook of the Legion of Mary. Dublin: Concilium Legionis Mariae, 2005.

GUADALUPE

Carroll, Warren H. *Our Lady of Guadalupe and the Conquest of Darkness*. Front Royal, VA: Christendom Publications, 1983.

A Handbook on Guadalupe. New Bedford, MA: Academy of the Immaculate, 2001.

Johnston, Francis. *The Wonder of Guadalupe: The Origin and Cult of the Miraculous Image of the Blessed Virgin in Mexico*. Rockford, IL: Tan Books, 1981.

FATIMA

Marchi, John de. *Fatima, the Facts*. Trans., I.M. Kingsbury. Cork, Ireland: Mercier, 1950.

Fox, Robert J., Antonio Maria Martins, and Maria Lucia Irmal. *Documents on Fatima and the Memoirs of Sister Lucia*. Waite Park, MN: Fatima Family Apostolate, 2002.

ST. MAXIMILIAN KOLBE

Bartosik, Grzegorz M., "Rapporto fra la Spirito Santo e Maria come principio della mediazione mariana negli ultimi scritti (1935–1941) di San Massimiliano Maria Kolbe." *Miles Immaculatae* 27 (1991): 244–268.

Bignami, Rosella. "Fr. Luigi Faccenda, O.F.M., Conv., and the Kolbean Marian and Missionary Charism." *Marian Studies* 54 (2003): 146–155.

Kalvelage, Francis M., ed. *Kolbe: Saint of the Immaculate*. New Bedford, MA: Franciscans of the Immaculate, 2001.

Kolbe, St. Maximilian. "The Ideals and Program of The Knights of the Immaculata: (International Latin name: Militia Immaculatae or "MI") in the words of its Founder: A brochure for distribution among priests by Niepokalanow in 1938." Translated by Bernard Geiger. Consecration: Militia of the Immaculata. http://www.consecration.com/default. aspx?id=33.

Piacenti, Ernesto. *Dottrina mariologica del P. Massimiliano Kolbe: Ricostruzione e Valutazione Critico-Comparativa con la mariologia prima e dopo il Vaticano II.* Roma: Herder, 1971.

————. *Panorama of the Marian Doctrine of Bl. Maximilian Kolbe.* Translated by Donald Kos. Kenosha, WI: Franciscan Marytown Press, 1975.

Simbula, Giuseppe. "Lo Spirito Santo nell'esperienza spirituale e nella riflessione teologica di S. Massimiliano Kolbe." *Miles Immaculatae* 33 (1997): 455–492.

SACRIFICE FOR SINNERS

Our Lady of Fatima's Summons to Sacrifice for Sinners as Exemplified by Saint Maximilian Maria Kolbe

Monsignor Charles M. Mangan

Introduction

Perhaps the best known element of Our Lady's requests at Fatima is her insistence on prayer, which is very vital to the message of Fatima.[1] Our Lady lost no time in exhorting the three shepherd children to pray, especially the Most Holy Rosary.

An outgrowth of our prayer is the newness of life that we experience. Prayer helps us to live with renewed meaning—a freshness and a corresponding vigor.

What is less recalled about the message of Fatima is Our Lady's summons to sacrifice, which is closely aligned to her call to make reparation for our sins and those of others. Here, we address "the daily duty." To do our daily duty is to pray and act according to our vocation. Our daily duty is performed under the banner of our trust in God. It is also done in acknowledgement of the obligation to repair for our sins. As friends of God, we ache when he and his justice have been offended. We want to "make right" when Our Lord has been disrespected.

---

[1] There are many excellent volumes devoted to informing and inspiring readers about the Mother of God and her appearances at Fatima. A recent and useful work is *Fatima for Today: The Urgent Marian Message of Hope* by the Reverend Andrew Apostoli, C.F.R. (San Francisco: Ignatius Press, 2010). Although there is no *imprimatur*, this book carries a Foreword by Raymond Leo Cardinal Burke, the Archbishop Emeritus of Saint Louis and the former Prefect of the Supreme Tribunal of the Apostolic Signatura.

Father Robert Joseph Fox, the late Founder and the Director of the Fatima Family Apostolate, when asked whether the Warner Brothers film about Our Lady of Fatima from the 1950's was a good presentation of the Fatima message—responded that, while it was a helpful introduction, it did not sufficiently address the importance of sacrifice.[2]

The Angel Came in 1916

Any discussion of Our Lady's visits of 1917 near Fatima to Lucia dos Santos (1907–2005), Francisco Marto (1908–1919) and Jacinta Marto (1910–1920), should be preceded with reference to the 1916 appearances of the Angel at the Loca do Cabeço, which was a tiny impression near Fatima. The Angel identified himself to the trio as the "Angel of Peace" and the "Guardian Angel of Portugal."

The three visits of the Angel occurred in the spring, the summer and the autumn of that year. While "tilling the soil" for Our Blessed Mother's subsequent appearances, the Angel emphasized to the three shepherd children the importance of prayer and sacrifice, the Real Presence of Christ in the Most Blessed Sacrament and the reparation to be offered to It.

And in that second apparition, the Angel was not finished giving counsel:

> Make of everything you can a sacrifice, and offer it to God as an act of reparation for the sins by which He is offended, and in supplication for the conversion of sinners. You will thus draw down peace upon your country. I am its Angel Guardian, the Angel of Portugal. Above all, accept and bear with submission, the suffering which the Lord will send you.[3]

---

2 As told by Father Fox to the author of this essay.

3 Lucia dos Santos (Sister Lucia), *Fatima in Lucia's Own Words: Sister Lucia's Memoirs*, ed. Father Luis Kondor, S.D.V., trans. Dominican Nuns of Perpetual Rosary (Fatima: Postulation Centre, 1976), 152. Quoted in Apostoli, 27.

Our Lady's Visits of 1917

In the first apparition of Our Lady at Fatima, which was Sunday, May 13, 1917, Mary speaks clearly about sacrifice. The Ever-Virgin questioned the children: "Are you willing to offer yourselves to God and bear all the sufferings He wills to send you, as an act of reparation for the sins by which He is offended, and of supplication for the conversion of sinners?" The children responded, "Yes, we are willing." "Then you are going to have much to suffer, but the grace of God will be your comfort." Enveloped by an intense light that emanated from Mary's open hands, the children felt compelled to kneel, and they prayed: "O Most Holy Trinity, I adore You! My God, my God, I love You in the Most Blessed Sacrament!"[4]

What is perhaps most remembered about Our Lady's third apparition at Fatima, which was Friday, July 13, is Mary's mention of Hell. Less recalled is that before she spoke of Hell, Our Lady returned again to the theme of sacrifice. About four thousand people were present for this apparition. Mary informed the children that they should specifically recite the Most Holy Rosary in honor of "Our Lady of the Rosary." Before the trio saw a very frightening vision of Hell, Our Blessed Mother encouraged them:

> Sacrifice yourselves for sinners, and say many times, especially whenever you make any sacrifice: "O Jesus, it is for love of You, for the conversion of sinners, and in reparation for the sins committed against the Immaculate Heart of Mary."[5]

After the vision of Hell, Our Lady presented the "decade prayer," which is recited after each Mystery of the Most Holy Rosary:

> O my Jesus, forgive us, save us from the fire of Hell. Lead all souls to Heaven, especially those who are most in need.[6]

In the fourth apparition of Our Lady at Fatima, which was Sunday, August 19, she referred again to sacrifice. Six to eighteen thousand people went to the Cova on August 13, but the children were detained in jail by the Administrator of Villa Nova de Ourém.

---

4   Ibid., 158. Cf. Apostoli, 46–48.

5   Ibid., 162. Quoted in Apostoli, 58.

6   Ibid., 166. Quoted in Apostoli, 66.

When Mary's apparition happened on August 19, Our Lady indicated that the impending miracle, slated for October, would have been grander had the Administrator refrained from harassing the trio. Lucia was given instructions as to what to do with the money that visitors had left at the Cova. She asked for various cures for the suffering. Before departing, Our Blessed Mother said:

> Pray, pray very much. Make sacrifices for sinners. Many souls go to Hell, because no one is willing to help them with sacrifice.[7]

In the fifth apparition of Our Lady at Fatima, which was Friday, September 13, Our Lady spoke of sacrifice. About thirty thousand were in attendance for the briefest of the six apparitions. Our Lady set the stage for the October apparition:

> In October Our Lord will come, as well as Our Lady of Dolors and Our Lady of Mount Carmel. Saint Joseph will appear with the Child Jesus to bless the world.[8]

Mary also compassionately addressed the subject of the generous acts of self-denial that the children were performing.

> God is pleased with your sacrifices. He does not want you to sleep with the rope on (tied around the waist), but only to wear it during the daytime.[9]

What we have just seen is the emphasis on sacrifice that Our Lady gave at Fatima. This stress on sacrifice for sinners is combined with Mary's invitation to pray, wear her Brown Scapular and perform one's daily duty.

This message of Fatima is good news to be shared. There are many Catholics who are still unaware of Our Lady of Fatima and her message. There is still a lot of work to be done today. There is so much we can do in our families and our parishes to promote Our Lady and her words to the children. We can recite the Most Holy Rosary at home. We can ask our pastor for permission to pray the Most Holy Rosary in our parish church before or after

---

7 Ibid., 167. Quoted in Apostoli, 107.

8 Ibid., 168. Quoted in Apostoli, 111.

9 Ibid. Quoted in Apostoli, 113.

Holy Mass. We can present the Brown Scapular of Our Lady of Mount Carmel to the children and help educate them in this great gift. And especially, we can seek to evangelize effectively by living the Fatima message, i.e., by praying the Rosary, receiving the Sacraments of the Church, reciting the various prayers we have been taught throughout our lives, wearing the Brown Scapular of Our Lady of Mount Carmel, and performing our daily duty. This is the summons to sacrifice for sinners that Our Lady uttered at Fatima.

Pope Benedict XVI spoke about our response to the message of Fatima during his own pilgrimage to Fatima that occurred on May 11–14, 2010, in commemoration of the Tenth Anniversary of the beatification of two of the little shepherds of Fatima, Jacinta and Francisco:

> The important thing is that that message, the response of Fatima, in substance is not directed to particular devotions, but precisely to the fundamental response, that is to ongoing conversion, prayer, penance, and the three theological virtues: faith, hope, and charity. Thus we see here, the true fundamental response which the Church must give—which we, every one of us, must give in this situation. As for the new things we can find in this message today, there is also the fact that the attacks on the Pope and the Church come not only from without, but the sufferings of the Church come precisely from within the Church, from the sin existing within the Church. This too is something that we have always known, but today we are seeing it in a really terrifying way: the greatest persecution of the Church, comes not from her enemies without, but arises from sin within the Church, and that the Church thus has a deep need to relearn penance, to accept purification, to learn forgiveness on the one hand, but also the need for justice. Forgiveness does not replace justice. In a word, we need to relearn precisely this essential: conversion, prayer, penance and the theological virtues. This is our response, we are realists in expecting that evil always attacks, attacks from within and without, yet that the forces of good are also ever present and that, in the end, the Lord is more powerful

than evil and Our Lady is for us the visible, motherly guarantee of God's goodness, which is always the last word in history.[10]

Fatima is about loving God and hearing and responding to Mary's summons to sacrifice for sinners. We must want to do all we can in responding to Our Lady. We do not want to disappoint her and her Divine Son, but to live as the Two Hearts desire.

The Fatima message is the message that continues to resound today. Since 1917, there have been incredible witnesses to the message of Fatima who have lived this message with vigor and truth.

Saint Maximilian Maria Kolbe: Witness to Our Lady

Saint Maximilian Maria Kolbe (1894–1941) lived the summons to sacrifice issued by Our Lady of Fatima. The sacrifice for sinners was part and parcel of his remarkable life.

He was named Raymond at birth. His parents were diligent in practicing their Catholic faith. And each of them seriously embraced their vocation as the spouse of the other.

Biographer, Ann Ball, relates the following telling story, which has become quite famous.

> As a child, Raymond was so mischievous that one day his mother, in exasperation, asked him, "Raymond, what is to become of you?" The boy asked himself the same question, then went to church to pray and repeat his question to the Blessed Mother. Later, he confided to his mother that at this visit he had had a mystical experience in which he saw Our Lady. In her hands she held two crowns: a white one for purity and a red one for martyrdom. "Which do you choose?" the apparition seemed to say. Raymond's heart leaped as he answered, "I choose both." Silently Our Lady smiled approval of the choice and faded from view.[11]

---

10 Pope Benedict XVI, "Meeting of His Holiness Benedict XVI with journalists during the flight to Lisbon," May 11, 2010 (http://w2.vatican.va/content/benedict-xvi/en/speeches/2010/may/documents/hf_ben-xvi_spe_20100511_portogallo-interview.html).

11 Ann Ball, "Saint Maximilian Kolbe," in *Modern Saints: Their Lives and Faces*, Book One (Rockford, Illinois: Tan Books and Publishers, Inc., 1983), 353.

Raymond was an excellent student who loved mathematics and physics[12] along with philosophy and theology. He also had interest in military affairs.

Once the dream of being a great military solider died down, he saw a new cause on the horizon. Spiritual union with God through Mary would then bring permanent joy to him and become the passion of his life.

Raymond was eventually accepted into the Conventual Franciscans. On September 4, 1910, he was invested in the Franciscan habit and took the name, "Maximilian."

As a seminarian, he studied philosophy and theology in Rome. The desire to be a solider continued, but now not as a member of the army but as a warrior for Christ.

He experienced the world during times of immense evil. The fight, Brother Maximilian Maria realized, was in reality a spiritual one, which demanded much from anyone who was willing to partake in it.

On October 16, 1917, three days after Our Lady's final appearance that year at Fatima during which the sun spun, he and six others founded the crusade of Mary Immaculate (*Militia Immaculatae*). He aimed to convert sinners, particularly Freemasons, heretics and schismatics. How he desired for all men to love Mary Immaculate! He possessed deep love for all persons, whom he desperately wanted to lead to Heaven.

Having been ordained in 1918, Father Maximilian Maria left Rome and returned to Poland. Upon returning, he saw that his country was once again free from external powers. He attributed the liberation of his fatherland to Mary Immaculate.

The year 1920 was the stage for a heavy cross: Father Maximilian Maria suffered from chronic tuberculosis. He spent the next two years in a sanatorium. But he did not lose hope, as evidenced by his words:

---

[12] Cf. Ibid., Young Raymond even "sketched many plans for rocket ships, and while a student in Rome, actually designed a spacecraft and applied for a patent on it."

The Immaculate Virgin will maintain her victory over the devil, and to make this victory ever more imposing, she will take us to her service, us weak ones with our not especially qualified talents.[13]

And he acknowledged the perilous era and what was at stake:

Modern times are dominated by Satan and will be more so in the future. The conflict with Hell cannot be engaged by men, even the most clever. The Immaculata alone has from God the promise of victory over Satan.[14]

Father Kolbe wanted to conquer souls for Christ through Mary. He assisted in Krakow with the publishing of the magazine, *The Knight of the Immaculate*. Funds were scarce, and skeptics were convinced that this project was doomed from the beginning. Yet, his journalistic efforts were fruitful beyond imagining.[15]

In the early 1930s, this Conventual Franciscan traveled to Japan and became a missionary. He especially assisted non-Christians in coming to appreciate Jesus Christ and His Ever-Virgin Mother.

As Father Maximilian Maria envisioned performing magnificent acts for God, these deeds demanded his physical well-being; however, that began to deteriorate while his spiritual well-being increased. Some believed that his "restless spirit" would not allow his good efforts to be confined just to one religious house or to one country. As he left for Japan, he was convinced that this was God's plan for him: to share the Faith of Christ with others around him in the vastly unique land of Japan.

Father Kolbe's passionate zeal to do all in the Most Holy Name of Mary stirred hearts. And he proved to be a true, wise and prudent missionary. He did not attempt to impose Western ideas on the Japanese, but knew his ultimate goal: to share true faith in Christ and to lead his listeners to Him. Such a goal transcends all national boundaries.

---

13 Ball, 355.

14 Ibid.

15 Ibid. "By 1939, the circulation of *The Knight* had grown to nearly a million readers, and several other periodical publications had been added."

Although the saintly Franciscan's physical health continued to worsen, he did not stop to rest but proceeded in faith, regardless of illness and decreased energy.

In 1936, Father Maximilian Maria was recalled by his Superior to Poland to promote Our Lady via the press, as he had done previously. Thus, he left Japan for the last time. In his homeland, he

> was appointed superior at the City of the Immaculata (*Niepokalanów*), and intended to continue with his work there. But World War II broke out, and almost immediately after the German occupation, this Catholic publishing apostolate became the target of bitter and increasing reprisals. Calmly, Father Kolbe assured his brothers, "The true City of the Immaculata is in your hearts."[16]

The end of his life was very near when the Gestapo came and took him from the Friary. He offered himself completely and gave himself for sinners. He willingly laid down his life in the concentration camp at Auschwitz for a man who was both a husband and a father. Father Kolbe's past sacrifices now culminated in this heroic act that eventually led to his martyrdom.

On August 14, 1941, the eve of the Feast of the Assumption of the Blessed Virgin Mary, his beloved Immaculata—Father Maximilian Maria Kolbe died at Auschwitz.

Now from Heaven, Saint Maximilian Maria reminds us of the importance of sacrifice. He is truly a man of, and for, our times. He lived in times of persecution and hatred for God, Mary, the Church and the Holy Father, the Pope. The diabolical bitterness that surrounded him did not tarnish his personality. Saint Maximilian Maria had a childlike, trusting nature, which is naturally attributed to Our Lady's complete influence over him.

What do We Learn from Saint Maximilian Maria Kolbe?

We glean much from the life among us of this outstanding apostle of Christ and of Mary.

---

[16] Ibid., 356.

1. He was a man of prayer. Saint Maximilian Maria began and ended his days with prayer. He loved the Holy Mass, and he spent countless hours in the presence of the Most Blessed Sacrament. He sincerely venerated Our Blessed Lady and always sang her stunning praises. He declared:

> Whenever a person, who wholly and unreservedly surrenders himself to the Immaculata, visits Jesus in the Blessed Sacrament, he dedicates his whole visit to the Immaculata even though by only one "Mary!" He knows that he affords Jesus the greatest pleasure, that thus she makes that visit in him and through him, and he in her and through her.[17]

2. He was a man of study. He was a tremendous theologian and Mariologist. Even today, scholars pour over his written words. His commitment to explaining Our Blessed Lady as the Spouse of the Holy Spirit and as the Mediatrix of All Graces has stood the test of time. Any modern attempt to discuss these two facets of Mary would do well—and seems well-nigh obliged—to consult what Saint Maximilian Maria left behind.

3. He was a man who proclaimed Jesus Christ, Crucified and Risen. This priest and religious knew well his identity as a baptized person, religious and priest. He tirelessly spent himself in service to his neighbor and the Church, being constantly aware that Our Lord had fashioned him into an *alter Christus*—"another Christ." He sacrificed himself for sinners throughout the entirety of his life.

4. He was a man who was approachable by all. No obstacle existed between Father Kolbe and the People of God. A child, a physically, psychologically, emotionally or spiritually limited person, a rich or poor person, a highly educated or unlettered person … all found in this humble man of Mary a listening ear, a real *father* who lived for his children.

---

17 *Aim Higher! Spiritual and Marian Reflections of St. Maximilian Kolbe*, trans. by Father Dominic Wisz, O.F.M. Conv. (Libertyville, Illinois: Marytown Press, 2007), 29.

Abundant Virtues

The Fatima message is not complex. Rather, it is simple and straightforward. Yet, we need God's unfailing grace to comply with Our Blessed Mother's entreaties.

I suggest four virtues evident in the life of Saint Maximilian Maria Kolbe that we, too, can—and must—possess if we are to live Mary's summons to sacrifice for sinners that she delivered almost 100 years ago to the three shepherd children of Fatima.

FIDELITY – When a man and woman marry; when a man is ordained to the Diaconate or the Priesthood; and when a man or woman becomes a consecrated person by way of the Profession of Vows, faithfulness is required.

Without fidelity to our personal vocation, we are doomed to fail miserably along the path that God has marked for us. But with faithfulness, we will meet the challenges inherent to our vocation.

Faithful to the conclusion of his earthly life, Saint Maximilian Maria is an exemplar of how to accept God's grace and strive for fidelity.

HOPE – Much of humanity has scarce hope these days. We seem to forget often that Christ has died, that He has risen from the grave and that He lives among us, particularly in the Most Blessed Sacrament of the Altar.

How we must remain filled with the hope that reverberates: *Jesus Christ has already conquered Satan and sin*! The meek and gentle spiritual giant under consideration was nothing if he was not a man of hope. Saint Maximilian Maria eagerly pined for, as we pray in the Apostles' Creed, "the resurrection of the body, and life everlasting."

PERSEVERANCE – Saint Maximilian Maria was truly "heaven-bent" in going forward to Paradise. He would not be deterred. And he did not complain about the suffering he possessed but instead tried his best to finish the work that the merciful God had assigned to him.

39

Neither should we be deterred; nor should we complain about the crosses that Almighty God permits us to carry.

The perennial question that is often asked: How can we be successful in life? We *will* be successful insofar as one day we receive Everlasting Life. To attain Heaven, perseverance is absolutely necessary.

Trust – Confidence in God is to undergird all that we accomplish. Without trust in him, we flail away in whatever we attempt.

He is with us and wishes to guide us in our endeavors. He is our loving Father who cares for us. Therefore, we surrender to him.

Saint Maximilian Maria acknowledged before all that God was his benevolent Father and Mary, his tender Mother. He did not relent in putting his trust in the Two Hearts—the Most Sacred Heart of Jesus and the Immaculate Heart of Mary.

Conclusion

Saint Maximilian Maria Kolbe lived the summons of Our Lady of Fatima to sacrifice for sinners. As Mary asked him for the supreme sacrifice, Saint Maximilian Maria gladly fulfilled her request.

Our Lady pleads with us that we live our *daily duty*. This Polish martyr embraced his daily duty. For that reason, this son of Mary remains for us a hero, an example, a challenge and a model.

Only God Himself knows if we will be asked to become "red martyrs," that is giving our very blood for the Church. Whatever the case, each of us has sacrifices to make. Therefore, at the very least we will be "white martyrs" who rend ourselves in service of Jesus Christ and His Chaste Bride, the Church. And how He wants to accept our sacrifices!

We want to imitate Saint Maximilian Maria by joyfully and courageously accepting the sacrifices that God asks of us. Indeed, Our Lady of Fatima has summoned us to sacrifice. May our generosity resemble that of this Conventual Franciscan.

Our Lady's message to us is as simple as it is timely: prayer, penance, conversion and reparation. What could be more straightforward? What could be more necessary?

THE VERTEX OF LOVE

Jonathan Fleischmann

Love's Mechanics

In the return of all created things to God the Father (cf. *Jn* 1, 1; 16, 28), "the equal and contrary reaction," says St. Maximilian Kolbe, "proceeds inversely from that of creation." In creation, the Saint goes on to say, the action of God "proceeds from the Father through the Son and the Spirit, while in the return, by means of the Spirit, the Son becomes incarnate in [the Virgin Mary's] womb and through Him, love returns to the Father."[1] The Saint of Auschwitz goes on:

> In the union of the Holy Spirit with her, not only does love bind these two beings, but the first of them [the Holy Spirit] is all the love of the Most Holy Trinity, while the second [the Blessed Virgin Mary] is all the love of creation, and thus in that union heaven is joined to earth, the whole heaven with the whole earth, the whole of Uncreated Love with the whole of created love: this is *the vertex of love*.[2]

THIS STUDY by Jonathan Fleischmann, VERTEX OF LOVE, was first published in the electronic edition of the *Homiletic & Pastoral Review* for the issue for October, 2012. In granting the Academy permission to republish in whole, the editor asked for no financial remuneration, but only for an acknowledgement of first publication by *H & P R* of this fine study, which the Academy gladly does.

[1]   SK 1318. All citations from the writings of St. Maximilian Kolbe in this paper, with the exception of the Roman Conferences, are abbreviated SK and taken from *Scritti di Massimiliano Kolbe* (Roma 1997).

[2]   Ibid.

Since the image that St. Maximilian employs here of action and equal-and-opposite reaction is taken from Newtonian mechanics,[3] specifically the proposition known as Newton's third law: "for every action force there is an equal and opposite reaction force," we can perhaps visualize the thoughts of the Saint with the help of the diagram shown in Figure 1. In the following paragraphs, I wish to meditate on this diagram, and to explain its relevant features in reference to the thoughts of St. Maximilian Kolbe.

Love's Equilibrium

The form of the diagram shown in Figure 1 is not found in the work of St. Maximilian. However, it accurately represents the state

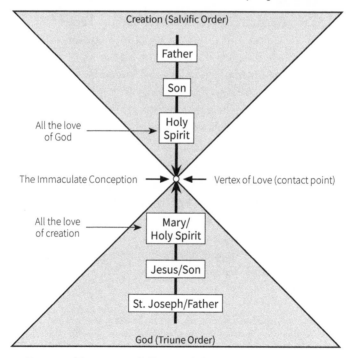

Figure 1: The return of all created things to God the Father.

---

[3] St. Maximilian liked physics. He once planned with one of his physics professors how he could build something like ballistic missiles that could drop packets of Marian publications on cities around the world more quickly than those items could be delivered by regular mail, which in the Saint's opinion was far too slow.

of equal and opposite action and reaction contact forces at a point of contact between two bodies. In this case, the "bodies" represent heaven and earth; the Uncreated and created orders; God and his creation. The first point I would like to make is that the state of equal and opposite contact forces in Newtonian mechanics requires "force equilibrium." It may then seem very wrong to use an image like this one because, how can the state shown between God and his creation be in equilibrium? Isn't God's Act of Love so much greater than the return of his creation that no "equilibrium" would be possible? This would certainly be the case if it were not for Emmanuel, that is, *God with us*. Jesus, who is truly man and truly God, belongs to both the created and Uncreated orders simultaneously. In His person, Jesus is both the Son of Mary, fully human and like us in all ways except sin, and the Eternal Son of God the Father, infinite and equal in all ways to the Triune God.

Thus, the love of Jesus, the Word made flesh who is God, is by itself enough to "balance" the love of God. However, there is even more in the equation of love's equilibrium than the love of the Son, infinite and sufficient in itself though it is. According to St. Maximilian, the perfect love of the Trinity meets an *adequate response* in the perfect love of the Immaculate, which is the name St. Maximilian gives to the Blessed Virgin Mary. How is it possible that Divine Love can find an adequate response in the love of a creature? It is possible precisely because of the name that the Virgin Mary can claim for herself. In 1854, the Blessed Virgin Mary proclaimed to St. Bernadette Soubirous: "I am the Immaculate Conception." In the words of St. Maximilian, the Blessed Virgin is the *Created* Immaculate Conception, as in the words of St. Bonaventure, and the Holy Spirit is the *Uncreated* Immaculate Conception.[4] The Holy Spirit proceeds from the Father and the Son as the Perfect and Infinite Love between the Father and the Son in the Eternal interior life of the Blessed Trinity. Thus, the Holy

---

4 Regarding the Mysteries of the interior life of the Blessed Trinity, St. Bonaventure said that the Son can be properly said to be "conceived," but only the Holy Spirit can be properly said to be "conception" (in *I Sent.*). St. Maximilian added the word "Immaculate" (perfect, holy) to the name given the Holy Spirit by St. Bonaventure, an addition St. Bonaventure would surely have approved.

Spirit is truly *all the love of the Most Holy Trinity*. The Holy Spirit is also called the Complement of the Blessed Trinity, because he is the completion of the Trinity, not in "number" (*quantitatively*), but in essence (*qualitatively*). When Mary, by the design of God before the creation of angels or the universe, and before the existence of sin or evil, was predestined in one and the same decree with Jesus Christ,[5] she was predestined to be the Spouse of the Holy Spirit, and so was predestined to hold within herself *all the love of creation*. Thus, St. Maximilian says that the Blessed Virgin Mary, then, "inserted into the love of the Most Holy Trinity becomes, from the very first moment of her existence, always, forever, the *Complement of the Most Holy Trinity*." We may paraphrase the thoughts of St. Maximilian Kolbe on the spousal relationship between the Holy Spirit and the Blessed Virgin Mary in the words of Father Peter Damian Fehlner:

> In virtue of this spousal union formally denoted by the title Complement, Mary is able to enter as no other into the order of the hypostatic union, her soul being wholly divinized,

---

5 The following is an excerpt taken from the Apostolic Constitution of Pope Pius IX *Ineffabilis Deus*, issued on December 8, 1854, in which the Holy Father solemnly declared the Dogma of the Immaculate Conception: "From the very beginning, and before time began, the Eternal Father chose and prepared for his only-begotten Son a Mother in whom the Son of God would become incarnate and from whom, in the blessed fullness of time, he would be born into this world. Above all creatures did God so love her that truly in her was the Father well pleased with singular delight. Therefore, far above all the angels and all the saints so wondrously did God endow her with the abundance of all heavenly gifts poured from the treasury of his divinity that this mother, ever absolutely free of all stain of sin, all fair and perfect, would possess that fullness of holy innocence and sanctity than which, under God, one cannot even imagine anything greater, and which, outside of God, no mind can succeed in comprehending fully. [...] And hence the very words with which the Sacred Scriptures speak of Uncreated Wisdom and set forth his eternal origin, the Church, both in its ecclesiastical offices and in its liturgy, has been wont to apply likewise to the origin of the Blessed Virgin, inasmuch as God, by one and the same decree, had established the origin of Mary and the Incarnation of Divine Wisdom." Here Blessed Pope Pius IX makes use both of the Scotistic thesis on the Absolute Joint Primacy of Jesus and Mary, both of whose existence were ordained before God's act of creation and before any consideration of original sin (cf. R. Rosini, O.F.M., *Mariology of Blessed John Duns Scotus*, translated by P. Fehlner, F.I., New Bedford 2008), and the formulation of St. Anselm, who said that Mary "shines with a purity greater than which none can be imagined" (*De Conceptione Virginis*).

because by the grace of the Immaculate Conception it has been "transubstantiated" into the Holy Spirit.[6]

It is for this reason that Mary, who, though she is a creature in both her person and her nature—is herself the Created Immaculate Conception and, therefore, *all the love of creation* —can actually provide an *adequate response* to the love of the Holy Spirit, who is the Uncreated Immaculate Conception and, therefore, *all the Love of God*. Thus, the equation of love's equilibrium is balanced again.

Now that we have balanced the equation of love's equilibrium twice over, we could certainly stop. However, there is reason to continue. St. Maximilian does not expressly mention St. Joseph in the context of these reflections. However, the diagram in Figure 1, based entirely on the Saint's own reflections, certainly suggests the presence of St. Joseph in the order of the response of creation to God the Father. The order of Father, Son, and Holy Spirit shown in the diagram reflects the order of God's loving Act of Creation, initiated by the zeal of the Father, designed by the wisdom of the Son, and effected by the action of the Holy Spirit. This is the order referred to by St. Maximilian when he says that "the equal and contrary reaction [i.e., the return of all creation to God] proceeds inversely from that of creation." We see this reflection in the diagram, where the reaction "force" of love is inverted, and the order of Father, Son, and Holy Spirit in the "action force" is reversed in the "reaction force" to give the order of Holy Spirit, Son, and Father. Notice, however, that in the return to God, it is *creation* that is reacting. Thus, the individuals reacting, while reflecting the Holy Spirit, Son, and Father to greater or lesser degrees, are all *creatures*. We have Mary, who is the perfect similitude (St. Bonaventure), transparent icon (St. Maximilian), or even *quasi-incarnation* (St. Maximilian) of the Holy Spirit, but who is still a created person, with a created human nature. We have Jesus, who is the Word Incarnate, the *same Person* as the Second Person of the Blessed Trinity, but who is still in possession of a created human nature. St. Maximilian stops here, but must we stop here? I would dare to say that the analogy we

---

6   P. Fehlner, F.I., *St. Maximilian Ma. Kolbe, Martyr of Charity – Pneumatologist* (New Bedford, 2004), pp. 100–101.

have carried out so far on the inspiration of St. Maximilian Kolbe suggests an obvious completion. We have St. Joseph, who has been called the "*perfect icon of God the Father*" by more than one saint.[7] In the words of Father Joachim Ferrer Arellano:

> In the light of the Scotistic thesis on the Primacy of Christ, to take one example, one discovers [...] how the virginal marriage of Mary and Joseph was predestined "ante mundi constitutionem" [before the constitution of the world], as an essential part of the one decree of the Incarnation of the Word in the womb of the Immaculate "ante praevisa merita" [before any consideration of antecedent merit]. Such is the saving plan, "the mystery hidden before the ages in God" (cf. *Eph* 3: 9), to be accomplished at the high point in the history of salvation. That high point is the fullness of time (cf. *Gal* 4: 4) when God sent his Son into the most pure bosom of Holy Mary ever Virgin, espoused to a man of the house of David (cf. *Lk* 1: 26) in fulfillment of the prophecy of Nathan. God acted thus, that through the obedience of the Spouses of Nazareth the Son might be freely welcomed into history on behalf of all mankind in order to save it. This welcome took place in the virginal womb of Mary, the Daughter of Zion, and in the house of Joseph, in the family home established by the marriage of the two Spouses [Mary and Joseph], "sanctuary of love and cradle of life." This is the theological foundation of the holy Patriarch's greatness as virginal, messianic father of the Only-begotten of the Father: shadow and transparent icon of Him who wished to make Joseph unique partaker of his fatherhood in order to prepare the human nature of Christ for the holocaust of Calvary. In this way, He made Joseph *Father and Lord* of the Church gushing forth from Christ's opened side and born of the sword of sorrow of the Woman.[8]

---

7   St. Theresa of Avila and St. Bernadette Soubirous are among these (cf. A. Dozè, "Le mystère de Saint Joseph révéle a deux femmes: Thérèse (d'Avila) et Bernadette," in *Actas simposio de Kevelaer 2005*), as well as St. Peter Julian Eymard (*Month of St. Joseph*).

8   J. Ferrer Arellano, "The Virginal Marriage of Mary and Joseph according to Bl. John Duns Scotus," in *Bl. John Duns Scotus and His Mariology, Commemoration of the Seventh Centenary of His Death*, Acts of the Symposium on Scotus' Mariology, Grey College, Durham – England (New Bedford, 2009), pp. 356–357.

In addition to being the transparent icon of God the Father, St. Joseph was the *true*, virginal, husband of the Blessed Virgin Mary.[9] In fact, it can even be said that St. Joseph is the virginal father of Jesus Christ. For, again in the words of Father Joachim Ferrer Arellano:

> Although singular, unique, and not univocal with fatherhood as this is ordinarily understood and commonly found among men, *the position more common and traditional* among theologians *upholds the truly real fatherhood of Joseph in relation to Jesus, based (1) on his marriage to Mary, the Mother of Jesus, and (2) on the right of the husband over his wife. He, therefore, who is born virginally of Mary, by reason of His birth, intimately pertains in some manner to Joseph as father.* [...] In view of the dignity of Joseph as husband of Mary to whom belongs the fruit of his wife's womb, one is not permitted to overlook [...] how the *indivisible virginity* of both spouses—not simply that of Mary, but also that of her husband, the son of David—is ordered to the *virginal fatherhood* of Joseph according to the Spirit, in virtue of the obedience of faith to the saving plan of God. This plan includes the *messianic fatherhood* of Joseph as son of David in relation to his virginal Son, constituted Son of David, the messianic King, because He was Son of Joseph.[10]

In the return of all created things to God the Father, it is under the leadership and in imitation of St. Joseph, our Patriarch,

---

9 Blessed John Duns Scotus and St. Maximilian Kolbe are both clear on this point, as are many other saints, including Saint Pope John Paul II (cf. *Redemptoris Custos*). The fact that Mary is the *Spouse* of the Holy Spirit, and the fact that their *perfect spousal love* results in Mary's *transubstantiation* into the Holy Spirit, does *not* imply that the Holy Spirit is the "husband" of Mary, or that the Holy Spirit is the "father" of Jesus. To approach an understanding of the perfect spousal union of love between the Holy Spirit and Mary, it must be understood that highest experience of spousal love, which is between husband and wife within the holy sacrament of marriage, is but an imperfect reflection of the source of spousal love, which is the Love between the Father and the Son in the Blessed Trinity, both of Whom in the inner life of the Trinity are, of course, without "gender" in the human sense of the term. This Perfect Spousal Love *is* the Holy Spirit, and it is as a fruit of this Spousal Love that the Blessed Virgin Mary is one with the Holy Spirit; transubstantiated into the Holy Spirit; the Holy Spirit quasi-incarnate. (cf. P. Fehlner, *St. Maximilian Ma. Kolbe, Martyr of Charity...*, pp. 102–115 and pp. 155–177.)

10 J. Ferrer Arellano, "The Virginal Marriage of Mary and Joseph...," pp. 385–386.

that the individual members of the Church must, by the merits gained for us through the Redemptive Sacrifice of Jesus Christ, the Incarnate Word of God, be *transubstantiated into Mary*, who is the Virgo Ecclesia Facta (Virgin-Made-Church).[11] It is only by being transubstantiated into Mary, the Created Immaculate Conception, that we can be united to God as she is uniquely united to God, being transubstantiated with her into the Uncreated Immaculate Conception, who is the Holy Spirit. In virtue of this transubstantiation, we are possessed by the Immaculate, and we are thereby formed into a single community or Church sharing her personality. To St. Maximilian, this is the *only* way that we can be members of Christ's Church, and thereby united to God. In the words of Father Peter Damian Fehlner:

> To this dynamic union of love in which not only the being of the Holy Spirit and that of Mary are united, but the entire love of heaven and that of earth touch, merge and become one so as to culminate in the Incarnation, in the birth of the Son of God, the Man-God, and then in the incorporation of the members of the Church into that Body conceived by the power of the Holy Spirit, the Saint of Niepokalanow and Auschwitz [St. Maximilian Kolbe] ascribes the fecundity of the Holy Spirit, precisely because Complement of Father and Son. [...] Whence the importance of Mary's possession of those who wish to be incorporated into Christ, conformed to Him in life and in death: *except through her it cannot be achieved* [emphasis added]. This mysterious, mutual possession, then, is the basis of all other cooperation in the work of salvation, the reason for rejecting the Protestant *solus* and "passive" ecclesio-typology, and affirming

---

[11] The title "Virgo Ecclesia Facta," or "Virgin-Made-Church" is applied to the Blessed Virgin by St. Francis of Assisi in his *Salute to the Blessed Virgin Mary* (cf. J. Schneider, O.F.M., *Virgo Ecclesia Facta: The Presence of Mary in the Crucifix of San Damiano and in the Office of the Passion of St. Francis of Assisi*, New Bedford 2004, p. 70). The phrase "transubstantiation into the Immaculate," though surprising, is used twice by St. Maximilian Kolbe to describe the *total consecration to the Immaculate* he demanded of his priests (cf. A. Geiger, F.I., "Marian Mediation as Presence and Transubstantiation into the Immaculate," in *Mary at the Foot of the Cross – III: Mater Unitatis, Acts of the Third International Symposium on Marian Coredemption*, New Bedford 2003), pp. 127–171.

the universal Marian mediation of grace or active ecclesio-typology.[12]

Thus, in accordance with St. Maximilian Kolbe's principle of action and reaction, what was first reversed in the order of God's Creative Act in the fullness of time, in the *objective order of salvation*—namely, that through the action of the Holy Spirit, Jesus Christ was incarnate of the Blessed Virgin Mary, and became man, and through Him Love returned to the Father—is reversed *again* in the *subjective order of salvation*: namely, that in imitation of our Patriarch and leader St. Joseph, through the merits gained for us by the Redemptive sacrifice of Jesus on Calvary, we can be transubstantiated into the Immaculate, and thereby form one Church sharing her personality; consequently sharing in her unique union with God in eternity, which is the Beatific Vision. This can be illustrated in the diagram shown in Figure 1, if one imagines traveling from the top of the diagram to the bottom, and then returning from the bottom of the diagram to the top again.

Love's Vertex

Our final meditation on the diagram shown in Figure 1 is the point of contact between heaven and earth, the *vertex of love*, where all the love of God and all the love of creation meet and are joined, and "in that union heaven is joined to earth, the whole heaven with the whole earth, the whole of Uncreated Love with the whole of created love."[13] This point of contact between the whole heaven and the whole earth is, according to St. Maximilian Kolbe, the Immaculate Conception of the Blessed Virgin Mary. Why is this? Why is the vertex of love not the Incarnation of Jesus Christ, the Son of God, who *is* Love? Indeed, the Saint of Auschwitz has been sharply criticized, and even ridiculed by some theologians, for what they have called a heresy along the lines of that of Joachim of Fiore.[14] It is claimed that, by making the vertex of love the

---

[12] P. Fehlner, *St. Maximilian Ma. Kolbe, Martyr of Charity...*, pp. 62–64.

[13] SK 1318.

[14] Joachim of Fiore was a theologian (c. 1135–1202) who de-emphasized the central role of the Incarnation in the Salvific Order. His theories were declared heretical at the Fourth

Immaculate Conception, the centrality of the Incarnation of Jesus Christ, the Son of God, is denied. However, precisely the opposite is true. For, in the words of Father Peter Damian Fehlner:

> Today this joachimite tendency generally reveals itself in constant anxiety about Catholic proneness to "exaggerate" Mary and a *downplaying* [emphasis added] of the active role of Mary in the work of salvation as Mother of God and Coredemptress so as to exalt the "mediation" of the Holy Spirit as principal "Coredemptor" (and for some "mother") of whom Mary is but the instrument (as are we), or so as to speak of the suffering of the Father. [...] But such trends historically have always been the prelude of unitarianism: not an affirmation of the Trinity, but its denial, a denial which must ultimately lead to some form of pantheism. [...] The significance of St. Maximilian's reflections on the Holy Spirit and Mary, and of his preferred terminology cannot be underestimated.[15]

It is the relationship of Mary to her Divine Son, which is the relationship of *Mother of God*, or *Theotokos*, which is the source of all her dignity, unparalleled among creatures. This dignity so far transcends the dignity of every other created being as to make her a "quasi-part" of the Blessed Trinity. It is in this very dignity, however, that the Incarnation of Jesus Christ is central, which is why St. Maximilian Kolbe's reflections on the Blessed Virgin Mary are directly opposed to the Joachimite heresy. Father Peter Damian Fehlner paraphrases St. Maximilian Kolbe on this subject as follows:

> Thus, Mary's self-definition is: "I am the Immaculate Conception." Only Mary can say this, because only of Mary Immaculate, jointly predestined with Christ for an absolute primacy in creation, can it be said that the whole world and each of us was made "for her."[16] Therefore of no other just person can it be said as it was said to Mary "The Lord is with

---

Lateran Council (1215) and at the Synod of Arles (1263).

[15] P. Fehlner, *St. Maximilian Ma. Kolbe, Martyr of Charity...*, pp. 82–85.

[16] SK 1305.

thee."[17] *For no other than the Immaculate can be Mother of God* [emphasis added]. Indeed, she remains only a creature; nonetheless in virtue of the Immaculate Conception she far transcends the supernatural perfection of even the greatest saints and of all the saints together, for as "quasi-part" of the Trinity she not only participates in the divine perfections, she is "inserted into the very bosom of the Trinity and into the order of the Incarnation."[18] [...][19] To be part of the Trinity, then, in so singular a way revolves about the divine Maternity, and by extension the spiritual maternity as well. For in loving the Immaculate the Divine Persons love us.[20]

In the famous Roman conference of 1937, St. Maximilian Kolbe defined sanctity with an equation: "S: v = V." The letter "S" stands for sanctity, the lowercase letter "v" stands for the will of a creature, and the uppercase letter "V" stands for the will of God. It is Mary Immaculate who is the perfect image, or icon, of sanctity, because it is only She who satisfies Kolbe's equation. "We may add with the Saint: perfect sanctity is perfect charity or Immaculate Conception."[21] This is the meaning of the vertex of love, and why that vertex is the Immaculate Conception, rather than the Incarnation. Mary is a *created person*, and yet Her will is *perfectly* united to the will of God: "v = V." In the words of St. Maximilian Kolbe:

---

[17] SK 1295.

[18] SK 1320; 1305; 1295; 1288.

[19] Father Fehlner continues: "While this personal communion or inexistence of the Holy Spirit and Mary Immaculate is absolutely unique in its perfection (a hierarchy or sacred order of its own kind), it is nonetheless the ontological basis making possible the sanctification of the Church as Bride of Christ, as sharing in the redemptive sacramentality of the Incarnation. This mediation of Mary qua created Immaculate Conception is the source of that mystical personality of the Church qua Bride, a personality of virgin and mother underlying and permeating every other dimension of the Church, including the petrine, hierarchical, sacramental-liturgical" (P. Fehlner, *St. Maximilian Ma. Kolbe, Martyr of Charity...*, p. 89). See also J. Ferrer Arellano, "The Triple and Inseparable Mediation of the Immaculate, the Eucharist and the Petrine Ministry in the Building Up of the Church Until the Parousia (The Three *Whites*)," in *Mary at the Foot of the Cross VI: Marian Coredemption in the Eucharistic Mystery, Acts of the Sixth International Symposium on Marian Coredemption* (New Bedford, 2007), pp. 41–93.

[20] P. Fehlner, *St. Maximilian Ma. Kolbe, Martyr of Charity...*, pp. 88–98.

[21] Ibid, p. 91.

The Immaculate, the Full of grace, as always united to the will of God. From all eternity she was in the thought of God who had willed Her so holy and perfect, to correspond with his will in a manner so complete. Hence, we can say that to do the will of God means to do the will of the Immaculate; and to do the will of the Immaculate means to do the will of God, because she is always united to God: *the Lord is with thee*; because she is always docile to the call of God: *be it done to me*; because she is always solicitous for the glory of God, always adoring, praising and thanking: *my soul magnifies the Lord*.[22]

We know well from St. Thomas Aquinas that love is in the will.[23] Thus, in the equation "$v = V$," we see that all the love of creation (in the will of the Immaculate Virgin Mary) is united to all the love of the Most Holy Trinity (in the Will of the Holy Spirit), and, in the words of St. Maximilian Kolbe, "in that union heaven is joined to earth, the whole heaven with the whole earth, the whole of Uncreated Love with the whole of created love: this is *the vertex of love*."[24]

Oh, sweet Heart of Mary, be our salvation!

Ave Maria!

---

[22] St. Maximilian Kolbe, in *Roman Conferences of St. Maximilian M. Kolbe, translated with introduction and notes by* Fr. Peter Damian Ma. Fehlner, F.I. (New Bedford, 2004), pp. 14–15.

[23] Despite the objections of Dietrich von Hildebrand (cf. Dietrich von Hildebrand, *The Nature of Love*).

[24] SK 1318.

THE MARIAN COMMENTARIES

**At the Incarnation, the Divine Word became as a creature,
and the word of a creature became as though divine.**

Fr. Giacinto Marie Dagesse

The Annunciation: *Luke* 1:26–38

²⁶In the sixth month the angel Gabriel was sent by God into a city of Galilee by the name of Nazareth, ²⁷to a virgin espoused to a man, whose name was Joseph of the house of David, and the virgin's name was Mary. ²⁸And entering he said to her, "Hail, full of grace, the Lord is with you." ²⁹But she was greatly troubled with his word and considered what sort of greeting this might be. ³⁰And the angel said to her, "Do not fear, Mary; for you have found favor before God. ³¹And behold, you will conceive in your womb and bear a son and will call His name Jesus. ³²He will be great and will be called the Son of the Most High, and the Lord God will give to Him the throne of David His father, ³³and He will reign over the house of Jacob forever, and of His kingdom there will be no end." ³⁴And Mary said to the angel, "How shall this be done, because I do not know man?" ³⁵And answering, the angel said to her, "The Holy Spirit will come upon you, and the power of the Most High will overshadow you; therefore, the holy one to be born will be called the Son of God. ³⁶And behold Elizabeth, your kinswoman, has also conceived a son in her old age, and this is the sixth month for her who was called barren, ³⁷for no word will be impossible with God. ³⁸And Mary said, "Behold, the handmaid of the Lord; may it be done to me according to your word." And the angel departed from her.

Teaching: *Lumen Gentium*, 56

"The Father of mercies willed that the Incarnation should be preceded by the acceptance of her who was predestined to be the mother of His Son, so that just as a woman contributed to death, so also a woman should contribute to life. That is true in outstanding fashion of the mother of Jesus, who gave to the world Him who is Life itself and who renews all things, and who was enriched by God with the gifts which befit such a role. It is no wonder therefore that the usage prevailed among the Fathers whereby they called the mother of God entirely holy and free from all stain of sin, as though fashioned by the Holy Spirit and formed as a new creature. Adorned from the first instant of her conception with the radiance of an entirely unique holiness, the Virgin of Nazareth is greeted, on God's command, by an angel messenger as *full of grace*, (cf. *Lk* 1:28) and to the heavenly messenger she replies: *Behold the handmaid of the Lord, be it done unto me according to thy word* (*Lk* 1:38). Thus Mary, a daughter of Adam, consenting to the divine Word, became the mother of Jesus, the one and only Mediator."

Meditation: *Anonymous*

"The Annunciation is of heaven and earth coming together. But, it is even more than this because through the Immaculate Conception that had happened already, but now, through her *Fiat* it is a greater participation and transformation. When we say *Yes*, all of us is transformed—into Him. When we receive Him, we believe that we are becoming Him. The more we become one with the Sacrifice—we participate in the Sacrifice—we become empty so that we can be filled. Filled with God who cannot be contained—is not stagnant—but flows through us to others. Through our thoughts, our actions, our voices. We stay 'nothings'—but that which flows through us is powerful... transforming. From the moment of her *Fiat*, Our Lady was already perfectly participating in faith, in the Sacrifice of this Gift who came to save the world."

Lk **1:26** In the sixth month the angel Gabriel was sent by God into a city of Galilee by the name of Nazareth...

Sixth month. The Annunciation occurred in the sixth month from the conception of St. John the Baptist. This may also, however, refer to the sixth month of *erusin,* the first stage of the espousals of St. Joseph and the Virgin Mary (cf. v. 27, espousal). If this be the case—a coinciding of their spousal consent with a miraculous conception—then it is wondrously illustrative of a principle given us by St. Lawrence of Brindisi *(Comm. Gen.)*: namely, that the chaste union of two wills is naturally (taken in a pre-lapsarian sense) fecund, yielding a conception or new life. Simply put: CONSENT + CONSENT → CONCEPTION. Such a thesis on the nature of man has profound implications not only regarding the spiritual maternity of the Immaculate, but also concerning its praxis in the lives of those who have consecrated themselves to her.

Historically, it was the sixth month, under the reign of King Darius, that the Israelites began to rebuild the Temple of Jerusalem, "the house of the Lord" *(Hag* 1:15). The Temple had been left desolate during the Babylonian exile, and its rebuilding had been vigorously opposed by the Samaritans. The name of the high priest during its successful reconstruction was Jesus (cf. *Hag* 1:12). *Typologically,* the building of the temple of the Lord's Body, His Sacred Humanity (cf. *Jn* 2:21), is announced by the Archangel Gabriel to the Blessed Virgin. With her *Fiat,* the Mother of Jesus clothed the Eternal Word with her Immaculate flesh. Thus we read, *Six and forty years was this temple in building (Jn* 2:20). Forty-six years equals the thirty-three years of Our Lord's life plus thirteen years, the age at which it seems most plausible that the Immaculate Virgin conceived the Christ. In the figure of the Temple, therefore, we see the continuity of Mary and Jesus in regard to His Sacred Humanity. The building of the temple of the Lord's Body, in other words, began with the Immaculate Conception of the Virgin Mary in the womb of her mother St. Anne. St. Andrew of Crete says as much in his sermon on the Nativity of the Blessed Virgin Mary: "This is, in fact, the day on which the Creator of the world constructed His temple; today is the day on which by a stupendous project a creature becomes the preferred dwelling of the Creator."

Gabriel. Literally, "Strength of God." St. Gabriel announces the Lord, "who was coming as the God of strength, and mighty in battle, to put down the powers of the air," namely, Satan and the other fallen angels.[1] "It was as a fit beginning for man's restoration, that an angel should be sent down from God to consecrate a virgin by a divine birth, for the first cause of man's perdition was the Devil sending a serpent to deceive a woman by the spirit of pride."[2] St. Lawrence of Brindisi sees the Archangel Gabriel as a "most honorable legate and go-between," sent to arrange the marriage of God and the Virgin Mary, just "as the matrimony of princes are accustomed to be treated."[3] In both Old Testament appearances, St. Gabriel is sent explicitly to strengthen the Prophet's understanding of the divine plan (cf. *Dan* 8:16–19 and 9:21–23).

Nazareth. "Christ was called a Nazarene, being, as it were, the country in which he was conceived. The Blessed Virgin therefore dwelt there with Joseph, to whom she was betrothed. The house or chamber in which she conceived Christ was consecrated by St. James and the other Apostles as a church. After three hundred years St. Helen built a temple there. Also St. Paula, St. Louis, and other travelers visited it. After a thousand years it was translated by angels from Nazareth to Dalmatia and thence to Italy, to Loreto, where it even now stands, and is visited by pilgrims from the whole world."[4]

---

[1]   St. Gregory the Great, *Catena Aurea.*

[2]   Theophylact, ibid.

[3]   *Mariale, 7th Serm. Annunc.,* 2.

[4]   Cornelius à Lapide, *Great Commentary, Lk* 1:26.

Lk **1:27** ... to a virgin espoused to a man, whose name was Joseph of the house of David, and the virgin's name was Mary.

Virgin. The Greek reads *parthenos.* The prophecy of *Isaiah* 7:14—*behold, a virgin shall conceive in the womb, and shall bring forth a son*—is cited in full by St. Matthew (1:22–23). Mary "remained a virgin in conceiving her Son, a virgin in giving birth to him, a virgin in carrying him, a virgin in nursing him at her breast, always a virgin."[5] St. Augustine links the Perpetual Virginity with the mystery of the virgin Church. He writes, "It was necessary for our Head by this mighty miracle to be born according to the flesh of a virgin that He might signify that his members were to be born in the spirit of a virgin Church."[6] The *Catechism* teaches the same. "At once virgin and mother, Mary is the symbol and the most perfect realization of the Church: 'the Church indeed... by receiving the word of God in faith becomes herself a mother. By preaching and Baptism she brings forth sons, who are conceived by the Holy Spirit and born of God, to a new and immortal life. She herself is a virgin, who keeps in its entirety and purity the faith she pledged to her spouse'" (*CCC* 507). St. Francis of Assisi, with true mystical intuition, invokes Our Lady as the "Virgin Made Church."[7]

Espoused to... Joseph. The Hebrew *erusin* ("betrothal") is the first of two stages of an ancient, Jewish marriage rite. Joseph and Mary are not engaged at the time of the Annunciation; they are, in fact, legally married. Although the espoused couple could not yet live together, the Mosaic Law safeguarded the marital goods of fidelity and permanence during this twelve month period: adultery was punishable by death (cf. *Dt* 22:23–27) and separation was possible only by means of a legal divorce.[8] Moreover, *erusin* is akin to a marriage *ratum non consummatum.* Marital relations (and hence the

---

5 St. Augustine, *Serm.* 186; cf. *CCC* 510.

6 *Catena Aurea.*

7 *Salutation of the Blessed Virgin Mary.*

8 Cf. Rashi, *Gen* 34:12, *Ex* 22:16; Targum *Pseudo-Jonathan, Dt* 22:25–27.

good of children) were proscribed until *nissuin,* the second stage of the marriage, when the couple finally came to live together.[9]

In the New Testament the Greek *mnesteuo* (*espouse*) is used exclusively in reference to St. Joseph and the Blessed Virgin Mary (cf. *Mt* 1:18; *Lk* 1:27; 2:5). There exists a yet even more pronounced singularity in the way in which St. Joseph "takes" Mary to be his wife in *Matthew* 1:20, 24.[10]

Mary. "In Hebrew *Miriam,* that is *Mar Yam,* myrrh, or bitterness of the sea; for the Hebrews have a tradition that the sister of Moses was called Miriam, because when she was born the bitter tyranny of Pharaoh in drowning the Hebrew children began. But, by the Divine will, the name was afterwards changed to a different meaning, for after the Red Sea had been crossed and Pharaoh had been drowned, she was called *Mariam* (*Mara Yam*), that is mistress of the sea; for as Moses was the leader of the men, so Miriam was the leader of the women in the passage of the Red Sea. Moreover she was a type, says St. Ambrose, of the Blessed Virgin, who is called Mary, that is the Mistress and Lady of the sea of this world, that she may lead us through it in safety to the Promised Land, that is, heaven. St. Isidore[11] says, 'Mary is by interpretation illuminator or star of the sea; for she brought forth the Light of the world. But in the Syrian language Mary is called Lady, because she brought forth the Lord.'"

"For this reason Mary was full of grace, and a sea of graces; for as all rivers run into the sea, so all graces which angels, patriarchs, apostles, martyrs, confessors, virgins possessed, came together in her, as St. Bonaventure says. St. Bridget also shows in her *Revelations,* 1.9, how delightful the name of Mary is to the angels, and how terrible to demons."[12]

---

9   Talmud, *Kidushin,* 12b; *Birkat Erusin.*

10   For a scriptural apologetic on the Perpetual Virginity of the Blessed Virgin Mary, cf. Word Study: *Paralambano.*

11   vii. *Etym. cap.* 10

12   Cornelius à Lapide, *Great Commentary, Lk* 1:27.

Lk **1:28** And entering he said to her, "Hail, full of grace, the Lord is with you."

Hail. The Greek reads *Chaire,* or Rejoice. This inaugural address of the New Testament is "an invitation to joy." It is the fulfillment of the prophecy given to Daughter Zion, called to rejoice wholeheartedly over her perfect redemption (cf. *Zeph* 3:14–18). "It was quite correct for the angel Gabriel to greet her as the 'Daughter of Zion,'" for she had been redeemed by her Son most perfectly by means of a *preservative* redemption, namely, the Immaculate Conception (*CCC* 722). Given Mary's profound knowledge of Sacred Scripture (cf. *Lk* 1:46–56), "it must clearly have appeared to her that she herself was the 'Daughter Zion' of whom the Prophet spoke."[13] "The Prophet Zephaniah, in addition, lets us know that this joy is reciprocal: we are invited to rejoice, but the Lord also rejoices in his relationship with us; indeed, the prophet writes: *he will exult over you with gladness, he will renew you in his love; he will exult over you with loud singing* (v. 17).[14] "Far different, then, to the news formerly addressed to the woman [Eve], is the announcement now made to the Virgin. In the former, the cause of sin was punished by the pains of childbirth; in the latter, through gladness, sorrow is driven away."[15] Surely, *there is cause for rejoicing here,* in every time and place. To this day among the Nicaraguan people (even the Protestant brethren), on the Feast of the Immaculate Conception one can hear "La Gritería," a cry of utter jubilation: ¿Qué causa tanta alegría? ¡La concepción de María! What causes so much joy? The Conception of Mary! Let us also make this, then, our spiritual exercise, never to let a day go by without rejoicing and giving thanks for the gift of our Holy Faith: that we have been given a right ordering—a divine *logos*—to our thoughts and desires; that we can understand, to whatever degree possible, the mystery of human suffering; and that the crosses in our lives can take on a resonance in Christ that other religions

---

[13] Benedict XVI, *Homily,* December 18, 2005.

[14] Ibid., December 16, 2012.

[15] St. Gregory of Nyssa, *Catena Aurea.*

simply cannot fathom. Rejoice with your whole heart that we have received this life-giving and saving faith!

A New Testament survey of *Chaire* reveals four direct parallels (present tense, active voice, imperative mood, second person, singular). Each is an address to Our Lord: three as "King" by the Roman centurions at the Crowning with Thorns (*Mt* 27:29; *Mk* 15:18; *Jn* 19:3) and one as "Rabbi" by Judas at the very moment of his betrayal (*Mt* 26:49). From this we learn the great cost of Christian joy, purchased for us by our dear Savior as the Man of Sorrows. Such a backdrop also perhaps provides an insight on why the Virgin became so *greatly troubled* at this greeting from the Angel: she knew well the prophecy of *Isaiah* on the Suffering Servant. And last, all this is said by way of introduction to the following remarks, which, although based on the Vulgate, are entirely in accord with the sense of the Greek reported here: specifically, the centurion's address of the Christ as "King."

The Latin reads *Ave,* or Hail. Historically, *Ave* was the salutation given to the Roman emperor at the time of one's death: *Ave, Caesar, morituri te salutant,* or "Hail, Caesar, those about to die salute you." It thus appears as a royal greeting. For example, in Scripture we hear the Roman centurions mocking the kingship of the Christ: *Hail, King of the Jews!* (*Mt* 27:29; *Mk* 15:18; *Jn* 19:3). Therefore, a royal significance may also be attributed to the Angel's greeting of the Virgin Mary. In this way, then, *Ave* is seen to be the heavenly proclamation of Our Lady's Queenship, a proper and royal address to the Queen Mother of *the King of kings*. This is the interpretation of the Church: "It can be said that the heavenly voice of the Archangel Gabriel was the first to proclaim Mary's royal office."[16] "The Immaculate will be, or rather ought to be, recognized as the Queen of each and every person, in… the entire world, as soon as possible. Behold our marching orders, for which it is worth living, working, suffering and dying."[17]

Moreover, *Ave* spelled backwards is *Eva* (the Latin for Eve). Hence, *Ave* may also be taken as a hailing of the New Eve, she who

---

[16] Ven. Pius XII, *Ad Caeli Reginam,* 34.

[17] St. Maximilian Kolbe, *Scritti,* 1127.

will effect the complete reversal of Eve's role in the Fall: i.e., Mary's faith heals the rupture of Eve's unbelief, the Virgin birth supersedes the curse with its pains of childbirth, and the Immaculate Conception supplants the Original Sin. And such is the faith of the Church in the ancient hymn *Ave Maris Stella* (c. 9th Century):

Sumens illud Ave	Taking that sweet Ave,
Gabrielis ore	which from Gabriel came,
Funda nos in pace	peace confirm within us,
Mutans Evae nomen.	changing Eva's name.

Full of grace. The Greek reads kecharitoméne. This heavenly title is the scriptural foundation of the Dogma of the Immaculate Conception.[18] "When the Fathers and writers of the Church meditated on the fact that the most Blessed Virgin was, in the name and by order of God himself, proclaimed full of grace by the Angel Gabriel when he announced her most sublime dignity of Mother of God, they thought that this singular and solemn salutation, never heard before, showed that the Mother of God is the seat of all divine graces and is adorned with all gifts of the Holy Spirit. To them Mary is an almost infinite treasury, an inexhaustible abyss of these gifts, to such an extent that she was never subject to the curse and was, together with her Son, the only partaker of perpetual benediction."[19] St. Jerome writes, "And it is well said, *Full of grace*, for to others, grace comes in part; but the fullness of grace in complete treasure was infused into Mary. She truly is full of grace through whom has been poured forth upon every creature the abundant rain of the Holy Spirit."[20]

---

[18] For further information, cf. Word Study: *Kecharitoméne*. Also, for a scriptural demonstration of the Dogma of the Immaculate Conception, cf. Word Study: *Dialogisomai*.

[19] Bl. Pius IX, *Ineffabilis Deus*.

[20] *Serm. de Assump. B.V.*

Lk **1:29** But she was greatly troubled with his word and considered what sort of greeting this might be.

Greatly troubled. The Greek reads *diatarasso,* literally "troubled through." Like *kecharitoméne,* this word is absolutely singular in all of Sacred Scripture; it occurs nowhere else. *Diatarasso* is also the first in a series of Marian vocabulary all of which begin with the prefix *dia-* or "through," a word-trend that highlights the Immaculate's role as Mediatrix of All Graces. Saint Bernard portrays for us how she was *greatly troubled.* "She was troubled, but not alarmed; her being troubled was a mark of modesty; her not being alarmed of courage; while her keeping silence and meditating was a mark of prudence."[21] And hear also the great St. Louis de Montfort on the Virgin's profound humility:

> So great was her humility that she desired nothing more upon earth than to remain unknown to herself and to others, and to be known only to God. In answer to her prayers to remain hidden, poor and lowly, God was pleased to conceal her from nearly every other human creature in her conception, her birth, her life, her mysteries, her resurrection and assumption... God the Father willed that she should perform no miracle during her life, at least no public one, although He had given her the power to do so. God the Son willed that she should speak very little although He had imparted His wisdom to her. Even though Mary was His faithful spouse, God the Holy Spirit willed that His apostles and evangelists should say very little about her and then only as much as was necessary to make Jesus known... She is the glorious Mother of God the Son who chose to humble and conceal her during her lifetime in order to foster her humility. He called her "Woman" as if she were a stranger, although in His heart He esteemed and loved her above all men and angels.[22]

Greatly troubled also connotes, as a kind of subtext, the gift of Fear of the Lord. Consider a verse remarkably concordant with the Annunciation, *Esther* 5:2:

---

[21] *Serm. 3, on Missus Est.*

[22] *True Devotion,* 2–5.

And Queen Esther said to him [King Artaxerxes], *"I saw you, my lord, as an angel of God, and my heart was troubled from fear of your glory; for you, my lord, are to be wondered at, and your person is full of grace."*

Here, being *troubled* stems from the *fear of your glory*. But understand from St. Bernard above how the Virgin's response differs essentially from that of Queen Esther, as well as that of the shepherds on Christmas night (cf. *Lk* 2:9). She is the Immaculate and thus suffers no inordinate passions.

Considered. The Greek reads *dialogisomai,* literally "to reason through." This word occurs in eight different contexts throughout the New Testament. Juxtaposed to the Immaculate Virgin at the Annunciation, the seven remaining passages stand in direct correspondence to the seven capital sins. In such a global context, *dialogisomai* indicates two significant findings: (1) the (nearly) universal scope of original sin in its specific effect of the darkening of the intellect (traditionally called *ignorance*); and (2) the absolutely singular and superior reasoning capacity of the Immaculate, who alone successfully arrives at the truth of things by the strength and light of her faith. Therefore, a detailed study of *dialogisomai* in the New Testament provides a *strong scriptural indication* of the absolutely singular privilege of the Immaculate Conception: that is, Our Lady's faculty of reason stands alone as having never been darkened by original sin and ignorance.[23]

Whereas the first interior movement of the Immaculate, *diatarasso,* concerns matters of "the heart,"[24] the subsequent movement of *dialogisomai* involves the intellect. And, the blessed fruit of this internal opus blossoms forth (dare we say, *spirates*) an act of the will, her *fiat.* Thus, the trinitarian aspect of the interior life—heart, intellect and will—is here evident. In any case, observe that the overarching focus is on Our Lady's interior, her personal subjectivity. For it is at this level that she participates most intimately in our redemption by means of her spiritual maternity.

---

23 Cf. Word Study: *Dialogisomai* for this scriptural demonstration of the Dogma of the Immaculate Conception.

24 Cf. *tarasso* in *Lam* 2:11; *Lk* 24:38; *Jn* 14:1, 27; *1 Pet* 3:14.

Also note that both *diatarasso* and *dialogisomai* point to her absolute singularity. That is, just as no one else in Sacred Scripture can be found to be so *greatly troubled* as she was, so too, no one may be found to equal her capacity to reason via *dialogisomai*. In a word, then, *diatarasso* indicates her Immaculate Heart and *dialogisomai* her immaculate intellect.

Lk **1:30** And the angel said to her, "Do not fear, Mary; for you have found favor before God."

Do not fear. "In fact, there was reason for her to fear, for it was a great burden to bear the weight of the world upon herself, to be the Mother of the universal King, to be the Mother of the Son of God: what a burden that was! It was too heavy a burden for human strength to bear! But the Angel said: 'Do not fear! Yes, you are carrying God, but God is carrying you. Do not fear!' These words, *Do not fear*, must have deeply penetrated Mary's heart. We can imagine how in various situations the Virgin must have pondered on those words; she must have heard them again."[25]

When a profound silence covered all things and night was in the middle of its course, your all-powerful Word, O Lord, bounded from heaven's royal throne (*Wis* 18:14–15). Such were the exterior circumstances of the Incarnation, and such also was the interior state of the Virgin in conceiving the Christ. All the faculties of her soul had been stilled in the most profound silence, the passions holding no sway. Hence, the Angel's reassurance, *Do not fear,* was as if to say, "That the King of Heaven may be conceived in you, this silence is to precede His coming." So also, in the prayer life of the Christian, interior silence is a *sine qua non* for a new advent of the Messiah.

You have found favor. This *favor* is the grace of the Divine Maternity. Listen to St. Louis de Montfort: "God the Father gave His only Son to the world only through Mary. Whatever desires the patriarchs may have cherished, whatever entreaties the prophets and saints of the Old Law may have made for 4,000 years to obtain that treasure, it was Mary alone who merited it and found grace before God by the power of her prayers and the perfection of her virtues."[26]

Particularly, the Virgin's humility is implied in the Angel's response, for we read, *God gives grace to the humble* (*1 Pt* 5:5). Thus, she fulfills perfectly the rule of the Wise Man, *The greater*

---

[25] Benedict XVI, *Homily,* December 18, 2005.

[26] *True Devotion,* 16.

you are, the more humble yourself in all things, and you shall find grace before God (Sir 3:20). In this light, let us endeavor like St. Gabriel to extol Our Lady. First, observe that Mary has *found grace before God,* and this is the supreme grace of her Divine Maternity. Second, given the singularity of *diatarasso* in all of Sacred Scripture ("greatly troubled," *Lk* 1:29), it is clear that the Virgin Mary humbled herself in a most singular manner, indeed, to the most extraordinary degree possible. It thus stands to reason from these two basic premises that the Immaculate must be the greatest of all creatures. By way of illustration, compare the following—the Old with the New—as if they were mirror images of each other:

a. *The greater you are*

b. *the more [you] humble yourself in all things,*

c. *and you shall find grace before God. (Sir* 3:20)

c'. Mary found the greatest grace before God.

b'. Mary humbled herself to the utmost in all things.

a'. Therefore, Mary is the greatest of all creatures.

And so with this one saying, *You have found favor,* the Archangel Gabriel confirms not only the Virgin Mary's profound humility, but also her ineffable excellence and exalted status over all of creation, even the angels. Our Lady is "Queen more than any other creature because of the sublime dignity of her soul and the excellence of the gifts she received."[27]

---

[27] Benedict XVI, *General Audience,* August 22, 2012.

Lk **1:31** "And behold, you will conceive in your womb and bear a son and will call His name Jesus."

Conceive. The Greek reads *sullambano*, "to collect, gather together" (literally, *to take with*). Like *diatarasso*, this is the first in a series of Marian vocabulary all of which begin with the same prefix: here, the prefix is *sun-*, "denoting *union*; *with* or *together*."[28] This word-trend underscores the Immaculate's role above all as Mother of Unity, she, who as the New Synagogue gathers into one the People of God. Hear the *Catechism* on this score. "Through Mary, the Holy Spirit begins to bring men, the objects of God's merciful love, into communion with Christ" (*CCC* 725). Looking ahead to Calvary, we find that this maternal *communio* with the Crucified occurs both at an ecclesial level (i.e., the four women of *Jn* 19:25) and an individual, subjective level (i.e., the beloved disciple of *Jn* 19:26–27). That is, Mary is Mother of the Church both in regard to the Mystical Body of Christ (i.e., corporately) and also of every individual member reborn in the waters of Baptism.

"The conception of Jesus in Mary's womb, in fact, is the prelude to the birth of every Christian in the womb of the Church."[29] Mary as "the Mother of the Church… now continues to fulfill from heaven her maternal function as the cooperator in the birth and development of divine life in the individual souls of redeemed men. This is a most consoling truth which, by the free consent of God the All-Wise, is an integrating part of the mystery of human salvation; therefore it must be held as faith by all Christians."[30] "In the womb of Mary the soul must be reborn in the form of Jesus Christ. She must nourish the soul with the milk of Her grace, lovingly care for it and rear it just as She nourished, cared for and reared Jesus. On her knees before Mary, the soul must learn to know and love Jesus. From Her heart it must attain love for Him,

---

28 *Strong's Concordance.*

29 Pope Francis, *General Audience,* September 3, 2014.

30 Bl. Paul VI, *Signum Magnum;* emphasis added.

or rather love Him with Her heart and become like Him by means of love."[31]

Jesus. Listen now to the beautiful teachings of the *Catechism* on the Most Holy Name of Jesus.

- "Jesus means in Hebrew: 'God saves.' At the annunciation, the angel Gabriel gave him the name Jesus as his proper name, which expresses both his identity and his mission" (430).

- "The name Jesus signifies that the very name of God is present in the person of his Son, made man for the universal and definitive redemption from sins. It is the divine name that alone brings salvation, and henceforth all can invoke his name, for Jesus united himself to all men through his Incarnation, so that there is no other name under heaven given among men by which we must be saved" (432).

- "Jesus' Resurrection glorifies the name of the Savior God, for from that time on it is the name of Jesus that fully manifests the supreme power of the name which is above every name (*Phil* 2:9–10). The evil spirits fear his name; in his name his disciples perform miracles, for the Father grants all they ask in this name" (434).

- "The name of Jesus is at the heart of Christian prayer. All liturgical prayers conclude with the words 'through our Lord Jesus Christ'. The *Hail Mary* reaches its high point in the words 'blessed is the fruit of thy womb, Jesus'" (435).

And on this last score, one ought to regard the *Ave Maria* as the immaculate invocation of the Divine Name, that which in the Old Covenant was held to be so sacred as to be mentioned but once a year, and that by the high priest alone.

---

[31] St. Maximilian Kolbe, *Scritti,* 1295.

Lk 1:32 "He will be great and will be called the Son of the Most High, and the Lord God will give to Him the throne of David His father..."

He will be great. "The greatness of the Savior... is diffused over the whole world. Go up to heaven, see there how it has filled the heavenly places; carry your thoughts down to the deep, behold, there too He has descended. If you see this, then, in like manner, behold, you will have fulfilled in very deed, *He shall be great.*"[32]

First let us consider the greatness of the Son of God according to His divine nature. The Eternal Wisdom, Who *orders all things well,* has diffused an impress of Himself in all of His works. Behold the beauty of creation! Surging forth from the depths of the ocean, the breaching humpback whale proclaims God's magnificence and providential care. In the vast expanse of the night sky, a shooting star blazes out but the faintest reflection of His seraphic Glory. The very intelligibility of creation itself—that man can even conduct the empirical sciences—testifies to the *Logos,* the Eternal Reason. God reveals Himself in nature, His theophany, and so *they have no excuse* who fail to acknowledge Him.

But, considered more closely, the Angel says, *He will be great.* He predicts a greatness still to be realized, and thus clearly cannot be referring to the inherent greatness of creation itself, for this has always existed, even from the beginning of time. And so, we must now proceed to the new creation and consider the greatness of the Son of God according to His human nature. For, just as the Eternal Wisdom has impressed all of creation with beauty—that is, the splendor of good order, or its own inherent *logos*—so, too, the created Wisdom now informs the new creation with a new beauty and glory. *And who is this... flowing with delights, leaning upon her Beloved (Cant* 8:5)? She is the Immaculate, the created Wisdom of God. Of her it is written, *He set in order charity in me (Cant* 2:4). She impresses the splendor of her own righteousness within those who are born of her from above. This is what we see transpiring at the Visitation in the soul of St. John the Baptist. Hence, Queen

---

[32] Origen, *Catena Aurea.*

Wisdom here truly asserts of herself, *My soul magnifies the Lord.* That is, her soul—and hers alone—"makes great" her Son in His new creation, the Church.

Son of the Most High. "The assumption of our flesh does not diminish anything from the loftiness of the Deity, but rather exalts the lowliness of man's nature. Hence it follows, *He will be called the Son of the Most High.* Not, 'you shall give Him the name,' but He Himself *will be called.* By whom, but His Father of like substance with Himself? For no one has known the Son but the Father. But He in Whom exists the infallible knowledge of His Son, is the true interpreter as to the name which should be given Him, when He says, *This is my beloved Son.* For such indeed from everlasting He is, though His name was not revealed until now; therefore He says, He *will be called,* not 'shall be made' or 'begotten.' For before the world, He was of like substance with the Father. Him therefore you shall conceive; His mother you shall become; Him shall your virgin shrine enclose, Whom the heavens were not able to contain."[33]

Throne of David. King David was grieved to see the Ark of God *lodged within skins,* while he himself dwelt in a house of cedar. He therefore resolved to build the Lord a house and received this promise: *He shall build a house to My name, and I will establish the throne of his kingdom forever* (2 Sam 7:1–17). *Allegorically,* when one takes Mary, the Ark of the Covenant, *into his own* as did the Beloved Disciple, he also receives the promise of the Kingdom, which has now come to *dwell in the midst of you.* As the Apostle writes, *Do you not know that you are the temple of God and that the Spirit of God dwells in you?… for holy is the temple of God, and this temple you are* (1 Cor 3:16–17). "Our Lord sat not on the earthly throne of David, the Jewish kingdom having been transferred to Herod. The seat of David is that on which our Lord reestablished His spiritual kingdom, which should never be destroyed. Hence it follows, *And he shall reign over the house of Jacob*"[34] (cf. *Isa* 9:7).

In the Davidic kingdom, the Queen Mother was seated upon a throne at the king's right hand. Her share in the royal power was

---

[33] Greek Ex., *Catena Aurea.*

[34] St. Basil, *Catena Aurea.*

thus unequaled beside him (cf. *1 Kgs* 2:19). The same holds true in the Kingdom of God with regard to Jesus and Mary. For, *all these things happened to them as a type, and they were written for our admonition, upon whom the final age of the world has come* (*1 Cor* 10:11).

St. Elizabeth of Hungary, despising her royal throne in the world, preferred instead the plight of the *minore* and the evangelical poverty of her Lord. Of her it may truly be said, *The daughters of kings come forth to meet Thee* (*Ps* 45:10). For her many exalted virtues and extraordinary love of the poor, she now enjoys an everlasting reign, triumphantly seated with *the King of kings* as victor over the world.

Lk **1:33** "… and He will reign over the house of Jacob forever, and of His kingdom there will be no end."

He will reign. Jesus conquers the heart of man by freely laying down His life for us in love. The greater serves the lesser, indeed, *becomes* the lesser, precisely in order to cultivate our loving trust, such that we might willingly come to Him. *And I, if I be lifted up from the earth, will draw all things to Myself* (*Jn* 12:32). In taking our sins upon Himself, the Lord willingly became an object of scorn and contempt for us. Behold, Christ your King, crowned with thorns! "Jesus… unveiled the authentic content of his messianic kingship both in the transcendent identity of the Son of Man *who came down from heaven,* and in his redemptive mission as the suffering Servant: *The Son of Man came not to be served but to serve, and to give his life as a ransom for many.* Hence the true meaning of his kingship is revealed only when he is raised high on the cross" (*CCC* 440). "Let us remember that Jesus on the Cross was proclaimed king with this inscription written by Pilate: *The King of the Jews* (cf. *Mk* 15:26). On the Cross, at that moment, he is shown to be King; and how is he King? By suffering with us and for us, by loving to the end, and in this way governing and creating truth, love and justice."[35]

Christ the King "is said to reign 'in the hearts of men,' both by reason of the keenness of his intellect and the extent of his knowledge, and also because he is very truth, and it is from him that truth must be obediently received by all mankind. He reigns, too, *in the wills of men,* for in him the human will was perfectly and entirely obedient to the Holy Will of God, and further by his grace and inspiration he so subjects our free-will as to incite us to the most noble endeavors. He is *King of hearts,* too, by reason of his *charity which exceedeth all knowledge.* And His mercy and kindness which draw all men to him, for never has it been known, nor will it ever be, that man be loved so much and so universally as Jesus Christ."[36]

---

[35] Benedict XVI, *General Audience,* August 22, 2012.

[36] Pius XI, *Quas Primas,* 7.

The reign of Christ involves also the Immaculate as Queen Mother. "It was through the Blessed Virgin Mary that Jesus Christ came into the world, and it is also through her that He must reign in the world."[37] *Typologically*, Christ the King has bestowed upon her *up to half of My kingdom*. That is, hers is the most sweet government of the Divine Mercy. Whatsoever she asks is infallibly granted to her. Whereas Christ has retained to Himself the meting out of the Divine Justice, for He is Judge of both the living and the dead. "If then, as is certain, the knowledge and the kingdom of Jesus Christ must come into the world, it can only be as a necessary consequence of the knowledge and reign of Mary. She who first gave Him to the world will establish His kingdom in the world."[38] "The Immaculate must conquer the whole world for herself, and each individual soul as well, so that she can bring all back to God. This is why we must acknowledge her for what she is, and submit to her and to her reign, which is all gentleness."[39]

"Finally, the People of God share in the *royal* office of Christ... For the Christian, 'to reign is to serve him,' particularly when serving 'the poor and the suffering, in whom the Church recognizes the image of her poor and suffering founder' (*Lumen Gentium*, 8). The People of God fulfill their royal dignity by a life in keeping with their vocation to serve with Christ" (*CCC* 786).

House of Jacob. The Fathers understand this saying as referring principally to the Church, the New Israel. "This kingdom in David was a temporal one, but in Christ a spiritual and eternal one, because He reigns over His saints here by grace, and in heaven He will reign over them in glory."[40] "By the house of Jacob he means the whole Church, which either sprang from a good root, or though formerly a wild olive branch, has yet for a reward of its faith been grafted into the good olive tree."[41]

---

[37] St. Louis de Montfort, *True Devotion*, 1.

[38] Ibid., 9.

[39] St. Maximilian Kolbe, in Manteau-Bonamy, *The Immaculate Conception and the Holy Spirit*, 105.

[40] Cornelius à Lapide, *Great Commentary*.

[41] St. Theophylact, *Catena Aurea*.

Kingdom. "The Law, the sign of God's promise and covenant, ought to have governed the hearts and institutions of that people to whom Abraham's faith gave birth. *If you will obey my voice and keep my covenant, ... you shall be to me a kingdom of priests and a holy nation* (*Ex* 19:5–6; cf. *1 Pet* 2:9). But after David, Israel gave in to the temptation of becoming a kingdom like other nations. The Kingdom, however, the object of the promise made to David, would be the work of the Holy Spirit; it would belong to the poor according to the Spirit" (*CCC* 709).

As Jesus Christ is truly said to be King, so, too, is the Immaculate truly said to be our Queen. "The main principle on which the royal dignity of Mary rests is without doubt her Divine Maternity. In Holy Writ, concerning the Son whom Mary will conceive, We read this sentence: *He shall be called the Son of the most High, and the Lord God shall give unto him the throne of David his father, and he shall reign in the house of Jacob forever, and of his kingdom there will be no end*, and in addition Mary is called *Mother of the Lord* (*Lk* 1:43); from this it is easily concluded that she is a Queen, since she bore a son who, at the very moment of His conception, because of the hypostatic union of the human nature with the Word, was also as man King and Lord of all things. So with complete justice St. John Damascene could write: "When she became Mother of the Creator, she truly became Queen of every creature... But the Blessed Virgin Mary should be called Queen, not only because of her Divine Motherhood, but also because God has willed her to have an exceptional role in the work of our eternal salvation. 'What more joyful, what sweeter thought can we have'—as... Pius XI wrote—'than that Christ is our King not only by natural right, but also by an acquired right, that which He won by the Redemption?'"[42]

In sum, the Queenship of Mary is founded both upon her Divine Maternity and her role as Coredemptrix. Thus we like to understand the Prophet: *For a Child is born to us, and a Son is given to us, and the government is upon His shoulder* (*Is* 9:6). First we read, *a Child is born to us*, and this is clearly so by means of His

---

[42] Ven. Pius XII, *Ad Caeli Reginam*, 34–35.

Virgin Mother. Such is the Divine Maternity. Next comes, *a Son is given to us,* and this also refers to Our Lady, insofar as at Calvary she freely surrendered her maternal rights to give her Son to us, for the life of the world. And this is the Coredemption. Last, we read, *And the government is upon His shoulder.* Such is the sweet reign of Christ the King. As the Good Shepherd, He lays down His life for His sheep, bearing them up on bleeding shoulders, unto the heavenly homeland. The Marian subtext necessarily leads to a similar conclusion regarding the *government* or reign of Mary as our Queen.

There will be no end (cf. *2 Sam* 8:13). "To reign for ever is of none save God alone; and hence though because of the Incarnation Christ is said to receive the seat of David, yet as being Himself God He is acknowledged to be the eternal King. It follows, *And His kingdom shall have no end,* not in that He is God, but in that He is man also. Now indeed He has the kingdom of many nations, but finally He shall reign over all, when all things shall be put under Him."[43] "To Him all things are made subject until He subjects Himself and all created things to the Father that God may be all in all. Now Christ has communicated this royal power to His disciples that they might be constituted in royal freedom and that by true penance and a holy life they might conquer the reign of sin in themselves. Further, He has shared this power so that serving Christ in their fellow men they might by humility and patience lead their brethren to that King for whom to serve is to reign. But the Lord wishes to spread His kingdom also by means of the laity, namely, a kingdom of truth and life, a kingdom of holiness and grace, a kingdom of justice, love and peace. In this kingdom creation itself will be delivered from its slavery to corruption into the freedom of the glory of the sons of God."[44] "Though already present in his Church, Christ's reign is nevertheless yet to be fulfilled *with power and great glory* by the King's return to earth" (*CCC* 671).

---

[43] Greek Ex., *Catena Aurea.*

[44] *Lumen Gentium,* 36.

Lk **1:34** And Mary said to the angel, "How shall this be done, because I do not know man?"

How shall this be done? "It was Mary's part neither to refuse belief in the Angel, nor too hastily take to herself the divine message. How subdued her answer is compared with the words of the Priest [Zachariah]. Mary said to the Angel, *How shall this be?* She says, *How shall this be?* He asks, *Whereby shall I know this?* He refuses to believe that which he says he does not know, and seeks, as it were, still further authority for belief. She avows herself willing to do that which she doubts not will be done, but how, she is anxious to know. Mary had read, *Behold, she shall conceive and bear a son.* She believed, therefore, that it should be so, but how it was to take place she had never read, for even to so great a prophet this had not been revealed. So great a mystery was not to be divulged by the mouth of man, but rather by an angel."[45] *I do not know man.* Mary's response indicates a prior vow of virginity. "Before He was conceived, He chose to be born of a woman already consecrated to God. This is the meaning of the words with which Mary replied to the angel's message that she was to bear a child... Surely she would not say that unless she had previously vowed her virginity to God. But because the customs of the Jews still refused this, she was betrothed to a just man, who would not take her by violence but rather guard against the violent what she had vowed."[46] Here observe that St. Joseph's virtue of justice revolves around Mary's vow of virginity. That is, St. Joseph is "just" precisely in that he upholds and defends the highest form of justice, the virtue of religion. Thus also, in the life of a Christian, true righteousness consists in defending Our Lady's privileges and, analogously, in safeguarding the purity and sanctity of Holy Mother Church in her teachings and her life. This is a call to a great nobility of spirit. On this, hear the eloquent Fr. Romano Guardini:

> Whatever is of a low order forces its way immediately; bodily needs, movements of defense and protection, essential

---

[45] St. Ambrose, *Catena Aurea.*

[46] St. Augustine, *De Sancta Virginitate,* IV, 4.

communications. The higher something rises, the more it loses the immediate force because it must pass through the spirit and the heart of man. The inmost being must open to it more and more purely. Very great and noble things have no immediate force at all, only their inner goodness and nobility. They appeal neither to natural urges nor to utility, neither to fear nor to ambition, or whatever the forces may be which arise spontaneously, but only to freedom, the depths of the heart, the heights of the spirit. Therefore they are wholly dependent on the responsibility of conscience and are defenseless in the world. Nobility consists in perceiving the voice of that which is lofty and consequently powerless, and in defending it.[47]

The saying, *I do not know man* indicates a prior vow of virginity for five reasons.

1. The first reason is contextual, as her question remains unintelligible without such an interpretation. "Hear the chaste words of the Virgin. The Angel tells her she shall bear a son, but she rests upon her virginity, deeming her inviolability a more precious thing than the Angel's declaration. Hence she says, *I do not know man*. These words of Mary are a token of what she was pondering in the secrets of her heart; for if for the sake of the marriage union she had wished to be espoused to Joseph, why was she seized with astonishment when the conception was made known to her? Seeing in truth she might herself be expecting at the time to become a mother according to the law of nature. But because it was meet that her body, being presented to God as a holy offering, should be kept inviolate, therefore she says, *I do not know man*. As if she said, 'Notwithstanding that you who speak are an Angel, yet that I should know a man is plainly an impossible thing. How then can I be a mother, having no husband? For Joseph I have acknowledged as my betrothed'."[48]

2. The second reason is scriptural and lies in the unique manner in which St. Joseph "takes" Mary to be his wife.[49]

---

[47] *And the Word Dwelt Among Us*, 22–23.

[48] St. Gregory of Nyssa, *Catena Aurea*.

[49] Cf. Word Study: *Paralambano*.

3. The third reason is grammatical. The literal translation of the phrase is, *Man I do not know. Man,* the direct object of *know,* is placed first to emphasize its universal character. In other words, Mary's "not knowing" must be understood as quite categorical, and distinctly so. None of the other parallels in Sacred Scripture are formulated in this way. Rather, in these passages the direct object "man" is placed last, as one would expect, and reads, *they do not know man* (cf. *Gen* 19:8; *Num* 31:35; *Judg* 21:12). By way of illustration, consider if one might say, "I do not drink alcohol." Such phrasing admits the possibility that I do not drink alcohol *now,* having since quit after many years of drinking. But if one were to assert in a most unusual fashion—"Alcohol I do not drink"—this more clearly underscores a constancy of purpose—inclusive of past, present and future—categorically never to drink alcohol.

4. A fourth reason is via concordance. Out of the four passages in Sacred Scripture in which we find a concordance of "know," "not" and "man," two of these involve either making an oath or swearing by an oath (cf. *Judg* 21:1–18; *2 Mac* 14:31–32).

5. A fifth reason is theological and follows by logical deduction. According to St. Thomas, "Works of perfection are more praiseworthy when performed in fulfillment of a vow, and Our Lady was most perfect."[50] She is most perfect, that is, not only in electing virginity as her state of life, but also most perfect in the execution thereof, viz., by means of the permanence of a vow.

Moreover, the extent to which Mary adhered to her vow of virginity is contained in the words, *I do not know man.* For revealed herein is the will to sacrifice even the privilege of the Divine Maternity, the longed-for hope of becoming the Mother of the Messiah. Indeed, she was disposed for just such an oblation, as Abraham had proven himself ready to sacrifice his only beloved son Isaac. And yet, trusting fully in the divine Promise, Mary gave her *Fiat* and became, beyond any natural explanation, the Virgin Mother.

---

[50] *ST* III, q. 28, a. 4.

In this way, Mary began to participate in the *kenosis* or self-emptying of her Son. On Calvary we witness the ultimate culmination of her obedience of faith, for here the oblation of the Divine Maternity is indeed realized. Freely surrendering her maternal rights, she sacrificed her only beloved Son for our salvation, that we might share in eternal life. Steadfastly *hoping against hope,* she became the Mother of the Church, bringing to full fruition the new life of divine grace: *Behold your son… Behold your mother.*

In all, we witness a depth of *kenosis* touching upon, as it were, the very identity of the Immaculate: an apparent self-annihilation through her simple and faithful adherence to the holy Will of God. Such is the apex of Gospel poverty, of *losing one's life in order to find it.* The itinerary of the Immaculate is this: from Virgin to Virgin Mother at the Annunciation, and from Virgin Mother to Mother of the Church at Calvary. Both moments immerse her in an apparent death-to-self. Both moments also, we should note, result in a conception through the obedience of faith. Having freely surrendered herself to the crucible of Divine Love, she brought forth—and continues to bring forth—the very Life Who is more powerful than death.

Lk **1:35** And answering, the angel said to her, "The Holy Spirit will come upon you, and the power of the Most High will overshadow you; therefore, the holy one to be born will be called the Son of God."

The Holy Spirit. The Holy Spirit is the Gift of Love of the Father and of the Son. St. Augustine arrived at the notion of the Holy Spirit as *Communio,* that is, as the very union of the Father with the Son. Complementary to this idea and equal in its theological import, is the insight of St. Maximilian Mary Kolbe: the Holy Spirit is the Uncreated Immaculate Conception, the very fruitfulness of *Communio.* From these two approaches on the nature of the Holy Spirit, two inseparable facets of love are clearly revealed—the unitive and the procreative—and situated within the life of the Most Blessed Trinity. With this as our foundation, we can now better appreciate the relationship of the Immaculate with the Holy Spirit.

1. Unitive: the *Communio* of Spousal Love

"In the union of the Holy Spirit with the Immaculate, not only does love unite these two Beings, but the first of these loves is all of the love of the Most Holy Trinity, while the second is all of the love of creation, and thus, in such a union, heaven unites itself with earth, the entirety of Uncreated Love with the entirety of created love: it is the apex of love… The Immaculate is united with the Holy Spirit in an ineffable way, by the fact that She is His Spouse, but She is so in an incomparably more perfect sense than this term can express in creatures. What kind of union is this? It is above all interior; it is the union of Her being with the being of the Holy Spirit. The Holy Spirit, in fact, dwells in Her, lives in Her, and does so from the first instant of Her existence, always and for all eternity."[51]

The spousal union of the Immaculate and the Holy Spirit may be called an *actual union,* inasmuch as they act always as one. With regard to the present consideration, this is the *communio* of charity.

---

[51] St. Maximilian Kolbe, *Scritti,* 1318.

2. Procreative: the *Conceptio* of *Communio*

"By the Holy Spirit's power and her faith, her virginity became uniquely fruitful" (*CCC* 723). "God the Holy Spirit, who does not produce any divine person, became fruitful through Mary whom he espoused. It was with her, in her and of her that he produced his masterpiece, God-made-man, and that he produces every day until the end of the world the members of the Body of this adorable Head. For this reason the more he finds Mary his dear and inseparable spouse in a soul the more powerful and effective he becomes in producing Jesus Christ in that soul and that soul in Jesus Christ. This does not mean that the Blessed Virgin confers on the Holy Spirit a fruitfulness which he does not already possess. Being God, he has the ability to produce just like the Father and the Son, although he does not use this power and so does not produce another divine person. But it does mean that the Holy Spirit chose to make use of our Blessed Lady, although he had no absolute need of her, in order to become actively fruitful in producing Jesus Christ and his members in her and by her. This is a mystery of grace unknown even to many of the most learned and spiritual of Christians."[52] "The Holy Spirit lives in the soul of the Immaculate, in Her being, and makes it fecund... This Uncreated Immaculate Conception immaculately conceives the divine life in the womb of Her soul, that is, Her Immaculate conception. The virginal womb of Mary's body is also reserved for Him, where He conceives in time—as all material things come about in time—the divine life of the Man-God as well."[53]

The Holy Spirit will come upon you. "In the Old Testament the Spirit of God is the power of creation; He it was who hovered over the waters in the beginning and shaped chaos into cosmos (*Gen* 1:2); when He is sent, living beings are created (*Ps* 104:30). So what is to happen here to Mary is new creation: the God who called forth being out of nothing makes a new beginning amid humanity: His Word becomes flesh."[54] The power of the new creation, the

---

[52] St. Louis de Montfort, *True Devotion*, 20–21.

[53] St. Maximilian Kolbe, *Scritti*, 1318.

[54] Ratzinger, *Introduction to Christianity*, 206.

Holy Spirit, also comes upon the Apostles at Pentecost (cf. *Acts* 1:8), for they will become the twelve foundation stones of the Heavenly Jerusalem, the Church.

The power of the Most High will overshadow you. Power refers to the Son, *Most High* to the Father, and *overshadow* to the Holy Spirit.[55] By substitution, then, we could rephrase the sentence as: The Son of the Father will Holy Spirit you. And again, we recall that the action of the Holy Spirit is twofold, effecting both *communio* and conception. At the Annunciation, this overshadowing of *communio* pertains not to the divine and human natures of Christ (for there are not two persons here), nor to the *communio* of the Immaculate with the Holy Spirit (for this was already realized in her Immaculate Conception), but rather to the *communio* between the Word and the Immaculate. And the nature of this *communio* will be discussed within the context of Our Lady's *Fiat* in verse 38.

Overshadow. The Greek reads *episkiazo.* In the New Testament, this word is found in the Transfiguration accounts and, after Pentecost, with St. Peter's very presence (cf. *Mt* 17:5; *Mk* 9:5; *Lk* 9:34; *Acts* 5:15). Whereas in the Old Testament the presence of the Holy Spirit prevents Moses from entering into the tabernacle of testimony, in the New Testament Ss. Peter, James and John are able to enter within the glory cloud, albeit with great fear (cf. *Ex* 40:35; *Lk* 9:34). Moreover, this verb, so strongly associated with the action of the Holy Spirit, is predicated of no other human being than St. Peter, the first Vicar of Christ on earth. St. Gregory the Great and St. Gregory of Nyssa understand *overshadow* at the Annunciation as referring to the assumption of Christ's human nature;[56] similarly, St. John of the Cross understands it as His conception.[57] The former underscores the unitive aspect of love and the latter the procreative.

---

[55] Cf. St. Gregory of Nyssa, *Catena Aurea;* St. Thomas Aquinas, *ST* III, Q. 32, a. 1, ad. 1; *CCC* 697).

[56] *Moral.* c. 2; *Catena Aurea.*

[57] *Living Flame of Love,* 3, 12.

The holy one to be born. Jesus Christ is holy in Himself—indeed, *is* Holiness itself as the Son of God. He is also holy in being begotten by the Holy Spirit, and not of man.

The Son of God. Each Sunday at Holy Mass the faithful confess in the Nicene Creed that Jesus Christ is *consubstantial with the Father.* Literally we are saying, He is "with-substance" with the Father. That is, the Father and the Son are of one and the same divine nature. The Council of Chalcedon (451 AD) speaks of this consubstantiality of the Christ in two distinct modes: Jesus Christ is "consubstantial with the Father according to the Godhead, and consubstantial with us according to the Manhood." And why, you may ask, do we bother to "theologize" in the liturgy about such an unfathomable mystery? Hear, then, whoever you are, the splendid reply of Fr. Lapide. As Catholics we confess Jesus Christ, "the Son of God by nature, Who would make all the faithful sons of God by grace."[58]

---

[58] *Great Commentary,* Lk 1:35.

Lk 1:36–37 "And behold Elizabeth, your kinswoman, has also conceived a son in her old age, and this is the sixth month for her who was called barren, for no word will be impossible with God."

Elizabeth. The Hebrew means "God is oath," a significance that will play prominently in our interpretation of the Visitation account.

Your kinswoman. "But someone will ask, 'How is Christ related to David, since Mary sprang from the blood of Aaron, the angel having declared Elizabeth to be her kinswoman?' But this was brought about by the Divine counsel, to the end that the royal race might be united to the priestly stock; that Christ, Who is both King and Priest, might be descended from both according to the flesh. For it is written that Aaron, the first High Priest according to the law, took from the tribe of Judah for his wife Elizabeth, the daughter of Aminadab. And observe the most holy administration of the Spirit, in ordering that the wife of Zechariah should be called Elizabeth, so bringing us back to that Elizabeth whom Aaron married."[59]

Called barren. The theme hearkens back to the type of Daughter Zion (v. 28). The new economy of grace, with its miraculous reversal of events, is presaged in Elizabeth's inexplicable pregnancy. Beyond all expectations, the barren woman, scorned and utterly shamed, is found to be transformed, blessed and greatly exalted as the mother of the Precursor.

Sixth month. St. John the Baptist is six months older than the Christ. *Sixth month* here forms an *inclusio*—a bookend type of structure—with the *sixth month* of verse 26. Thus we may see here a continuation of the theme there begun: i.e., the rebuilding of the Temple.

No word will be impossible. The Latin reads, *non omne verbum,* or "no word." God is always faithful to His promises. Always! It is the certain hope in God's all-surpassing wisdom, power, and fidelity that sustains Our Lady on Calvary, as she stands by the Cross of her Son. One of the more important doctrines on the interior

---

[59] St. Gregory Nazianzen, *Catena Aurea.*

life in this regard comes to us from the *Catechism*: "Nothing is more apt to confirm our faith and hope than holding it fixed in our minds that nothing is impossible with God" (*CCC* 274). We should, then, remind ourselves of this often. It is jet-fuel for the journey. "Inasmuch as with God neither does His word fall short of His intention, because He is Truth; nor His deed fall short of His word, because He is Power; nor the manner fall short of the deed, because He is Wisdom."[60]

---

[60] St. Bernard, *Serm. 4 on Missus Est.*

Lk **1:38** And Mary said, "Behold, the handmaid of the Lord; may it be done to me according to your word." And the angel departed from her.

Handmaid. "She is lowly: her only desire is to be the handmaid of the Lord. She knows that she will only contribute to the salvation of the world if, rather than carrying out her own projects, she places herself completely at the disposal of God's initiatives."[61] Such is the absolute trust of the Immaculate, "a young woman called to stake everything on the Word of the Lord."[62] "By entrusting ourselves to her prayer, we abandon ourselves to the will of God together with her: *Thy will be done*" (*CCC* 2677). Total consecration to the Immaculate allows us not only to participate intimately in the Gift of God, but also to become ourselves "gift." "She says to us: Take heart, it is love that wins in the end! The message of my life was: I am the handmaid of God, my life has been a gift of myself to God and my neighbor… May you too have trust and have the courage to live like this."[63]

"She calls herself His handmaid, who is chosen to be His mother, so far was she from being exalted by the sudden promise. At the same time also by calling herself handmaid, she claimed to herself in no other way the prerogative of such great grace than that she might do what was commanded her. For about to bring forth One meek and lowly, she was bound herself to show forth lowliness. As it follows, *May it be done to me according to your word*. You have her submission, you see her wish. *Behold the handmaid of the Lord*, signifies the readiness of duty: *May it be done to me according to your word*, the conception of the wish."[64]

May it be done to me. Mary's *Fiat* is the only perfect act of freedom made by a human person. As such, it presupposes the grace of the Immaculate Conception. Only she who *has been fully graced* is capable of making such an act. "If Mary's Yes had contained

---

[61] Benedict XVI, *Deus Caritas Est*, 41.

[62] Ibid., *Homily,* December 8, 2008.

[63] Ibid., August 15, 2007.

[64] St. Ambrose, *Catena Aurea*.

even the shadow of a demurral, of a 'so far and no farther', a stain would have clung to her faith and the Child could not have taken possession of the whole human nature."[65] "To be sure, Mary's Yes is wholly grace. The dogma of Mary's freedom from original sin is at bottom meant solely to show that it is not a human being who sets the redemption in motion by her own power; rather, her Yes is contained wholly within the primacy and priority of divine love, which already embraces her before she is born. 'All is grace.' Yet grace does not cancel freedom; it creates it."[66]

Just as there is one revealed Word of the Father by Whom *all things were created* (*Col* 1:16), so too is there one definitive *Yes* to this Word arising from all of creation—the *Fiat* of the Immaculate. *My dove, my perfect one is one* (*Cant* 6:9). Herein is the supreme *reditus*, the full return to God of all created charity. Thus, St. Maximilian speaks of a "vertex of charity." In this way, the Immaculate is seen to be the perfect complement of the Most Holy Trinity. That is, she exists in pure relation, or better, she *is* the pure relation— the *ad extra communio*—with each of the Divine Persons. First, in the order of being, she is the Spouse of the Holy Spirit as the Immaculate Conception. Hence, she makes the surprising self-identification at Lourdes, "I am the Immaculate Conception." Then, in the order of act, she is the Mother of the Son by virtue of her *Fiat*. Finally, on Calvary—the *Fiat* consummated and the *reditus* of love now fully accomplished—she is the Daughter of the Father, as it is written: *Be in pain and labor, O daughter of Zion, as a woman that brings forth; for now shall you go out of the city* (*Mic* 4:10); and, *Many daughters have gathered together riches; you have surpassed them all* (*Prov* 31:29); and, *As the lily among thorns, so is my love among the daughters* (*Cant* 2:2). Inasmuch as the word *daughter* in Sacred Scripture oftentimes represents an entire people, here we can associate "Daughter of the Father" with the title "Virgin made Church."

THEOLOGICAL. We have seen how the act of *overshadowing* of the Holy Spirit creates the possibility of *communio*, of entering or

---

65 von Balthasar, *Mary the Church at the Source*, 104–5.

66 Ratzinger, in *Mary, the Church at the Source*, 89–90.

being immersed in the divinity (v. 35). With this in mind, we now propose the following. With the overshadowing of the Holy Spirit, Mary's *Fiat* is assumed by the Word, analogous to the way in which Christ's human nature is assumed. The result is an *actual union,* comprised of two persons, now become one in act. Moreover, because of this actual union, the will of the Immaculate inevitably orients, draws and posits us within the Divine Will of Christ, that is, within the very marriage bond of Christ with His Bride, the Church. In a word, the Immaculate, and she alone, effects our communion with her Son.

Let us first consider that the assumption of a human nature by the Word creates two radical possibilities:

1. the possibility of redemption of our fallen human nature, and
2. the possibility of a sacramental perpetuation of Christ's Sacred Humanity throughout history in the Most Blessed Sacrament;

Then, it would follow by logical deduction that the assumption of a human act creates two radical possibilities as well:

1. the possibility of redemption of our fallen human acts via grace, and
2. the possibility of perpetuating this created *Fiat* throughout history, as the "unique formal cause" of our justification in Christ Jesus.

The idea merits attention as a real theological basis of the spiritual maternity of the Immaculate.

ASCETICAL-MYSTICAL. The memory of man is a "faculty" of the soul that attains to a *fullness of time* (cf. *Gal* 4:4). It aspires to synthesize past, present and future, the chronological succession of events, into a single PRESENT, or fullness of time. Now, in the soul justified by grace, the memory may be conceived as the seat of an abiding *fiat.* This personal *fiat* is the foundational act of the soul, by which it has cooperated with the prevenient grace of justification to yield its initial obedience of faith. This original act of justification, an appropriated and participated *fiat,* abides in the memory. Thus, we read in Sacred Scripture, *Truth has sprung up from the earth.* In its historical sense, St. Augustine tells us that this Truth is Christ Himself, who has sprung up from the virgin earth of the Immaculate Virgin Mary. From this we ought to learn that the Immaculate, *qua* Immaculate, just as she encompasses every grace—or rather, is a "sea of graces," as St. Louis de Montfort writes—so, too, is her memory continuously potent in this *fullness of time,* for there is no sin in her to hamper its full actualization. This is the first point to consider and from which we will base our understanding on what it means—and thus how to attain—to be immaculate as she who is the Immaculate. The following is a rudimentary attempt to portray this *active immaculation,* that in which the soul plays an active role.

Man, of course, is not free from the stain of sin, neither original nor personal. We suffer from concupiscence as well as from our own personal history of sinfulness. These, as in the Garden of Eden, constrict the soul in its full potential of being *capax Dei,* of being completely filled with the indwelling Presence of Christ. And this is specifically so in regard to the memory, in its capacity to effect the above-mentioned synthesis of past, present and future into the YES of a total self-gift to God and to neighbor. Now, this defect occurs in two basic ways, which have been recorded for us in the account of the Fall in *Genesis.* The first of these interior effects is the denial over what has happened in the past, over the sin committed. Here, there is introduced into the soul a radical "No" which, in the original sin is manifested by a transference of blame (cf. *Gen* 3:12–13). Such a denial of personal responsibility (for we have been given over to ourselves as *sui iuris*) is inevitably a radical denial of reality: a "No" to that which has actually transpired. This denial effects an expansive sorrow or pain of soul, the *sorrow unto death* of which the Apostle speaks, which, being situated in the memory as a past event, now aspires to draw man's entire personal subjectivity, past, present and future, into itself—into this NO, the content of which, again, is the nothingness of non-existence. The imagery of a subjective black-hole is certainly apropos here. In a word, this sorrow aspires to reign in the soul through a perpetual state of discouragement, the interior reign of unrepentant sin. To varying degrees, then, we see how Christ Jesus, the *Great Amen* in whom there is only "Yes," is not permitted to reign completely in this soul, insofar as His sovereignty does not extend—or rather is denied permission by the soul to extend completely over one's past. The remedy that must be diligently applied (even daily) as a spiritual exercise is to give our *fiat* to include the whole of one's past: all that has transpired in fact, whether for good or—in our limited perspective—for ill. *And as for these enemies of mine who did not wish me to be King, bring them before Me and slay them in My Presence.* Such is an *active immaculation* of one's past. It is the beginning of a radical liberation, of setting the captive self free from a state of perpetual self-accusation, as well as from unforgiveness. This we must do, *for God is greater than our hearts,* and *has loved us while we were yet sinners.* So much, then, for our brief look to the past. But let us be keenly aware of how the *second death* can begin in the soul even during this lifetime.

The same dynamic also holds true for the future. Here, there is anxiety, a vague fear of some impending evil, which can elicit from the soul a vehement "No" to its possible realization that such a thing may actually occur. Adam and Eve manifest this in hiding from the Lord God because of their nakedness (cf. *Gen* 3:10). Such fear is to be closed-off to the future, in truth, to be closed-down to the omnipotence, wisdom and goodness of God Himself. But here one must pose the incisive question of St. Paul, *What can separate us from the love of Christ?* In this wise, the soul must daily range over all these future possibilities like a sentinel on a watchtower. *Taking every thought captive for Christ,* our vigilant response must always and only be that of the Immaculate: *May it be done to me according to your word.*

According to your word. Mary believes the word of the Angel, whereas Eve had believed the lie of Lucifer. Recall that St. Gabriel means "the strength of God," from which name we see the rational basis of Mary's absolute trust: the omnipotence of the Lord Almighty, whose *word is full of power* (*Eccles* 8:4). Let all Christians now imitate the New Eve, for she is our Mother, the Mother of all the living in Christ Jesus her Son. Of her we may truly say, *Woman, great is your faith!* As the lie of the serpent first entered man through the woman, so now does the truth of Christ enter all men only through the Woman. And so, Christian, *Behold your*

Mother! Take with you words, that is, take in daily the inspired words of Sacred Scripture, as *a strong shield of faith against the fiery darts of the tempter.*

WORD STUDY: *KECHARITOMÉNE*

Who are You, *Kecharitoméne*? You are the Immaculate Mediatrix of All Graces.

"There is no fruit of grace in the history of salvation that does not have as its necessary instrument the mediation of Our Lady."

—Benedict XVI, Homily at canonization Mass of
Fr. Antônio de Sant'Ana Galvão, O.F.M., 11 May 2007

Abstract

The following word study of the Greek term Kecharitoméne—*"full of grace" (* Lk 1:28)—*brings to a scriptural light not only the truth of the Dogma of the Immaculate Conception, but also reveals the Immaculate as the Mediatrix of All Graces.*

Introduction

Full of grace: the Greek reads *Kecharitoméne*. Used only once in *Luke* 1:28, *Kecharitoméne* is as unique in all of revelation as the Immaculate is in all of creation. Even Origen, who knew the Bible inside and out, wondered at its singularity.[1] The term touches upon the very identity of the Immaculate, both revealing and veiling the mystery of her whom St. Maximilian continually and lovingly contemplated: "Who are you, O Immaculate Conception?" We now take up this question, beginning with its scriptural root: Who are you, *Kecharitoméne?*

This heavenly title is the scriptural foundation of the Dogma of the Immaculate Conception. "When the Fathers and writers of the Church meditated on the fact that the most Blessed Virgin was, in the name and by order of God himself, proclaimed full of grace by the Angel Gabriel when he announced her most sublime dignity of Mother of God, they thought that this singular and

---

[1] *Homily on Luke* 6, 7.

solemn salutation, never heard before, showed that the Mother of God is the seat of all divine graces and is adorned with all gifts of the Holy Spirit. To them Mary is an almost infinite treasury, an inexhaustible abyss of these gifts, to such an extent that she was never subject to the curse and was, together with her Son, the only partaker of perpetual benediction."[2] Part I of our study confirms this association of *Kecharitoméne* and the Immaculate Conception.

Part II examines the Old and New Testament parallels of *Kecharitoméne* and establishes a new correlation with Our Lady as Mediatrix of All Graces. St. Jerome makes this very connection, as he writes, "And it is well said, *Full of grace*, for to others, grace comes in part; but the fullness of grace in complete treasure was infused into Mary. She truly is *full of grace* through whom has been poured forth upon every creature the abundant rain of the Holy Spirit."[3]

Method

The spiritual sense of Sacred Scripture regards "not only the text of Scripture, but also the realities and events about which it speaks [as] *signs*."[4] This means that the literal people, places, and things of the Bible possess an innate potential to point to realities beyond themselves. Such latent power is one reason why the Word of God is likened to a seed.

> As a general rule, we can define the spiritual sense, as understood by Christian faith, as the meaning expressed by the biblical texts when read, under the influence of the Holy Spirit, in the context of the paschal mystery of Christ and of the new life which flows from it. This context truly exists. In it the New Testament recognizes the fulfillment of the Scriptures. It is therefore quite acceptable to re-read the Scriptures in the light of this new context, which is that of life in the Spirit.[5]

---

2 Bl. Pius IX, *Ineffabilis Deus.*

3 *Serm. de Assump. B.V.*

4 *CCC* 117.

5 Pontifical Biblical Commission. *The Interpretation of the Bible in the Church.* Boston: Pauline Books & Media, 1993: n. 85.

The early Church Fathers readily tapped into this spiritual sense via a kind of connaturality with the Word of God, the Greek language, and the gift of a prodigious memory. We, on the other hand, standing afar off in many ways, approach this spiritual knowledge most swiftly, securely, and beautifully through imitation of the Immaculate Virgin Mary, pondering the Word precisely as she did.

The first step of this Marian method is a "keeping together" of the Word.[6] Every occurrence of the word of study is gathered up from the Greek of the Septuagint and New Testament. For example, if we find that a given word occurs X number of times in the Bible, then all of these passages are compiled, "kept together," as it were.

The second step is "to cast together" this particular term with others related to it.[7] That is, associations are formed between it and others found to be prevalent within its immediate context. In this way, etymological trends are discovered. For example, two correlations of *Kecharitoméne* are observed to be "immaculate" and "predestination." Several such associations, interwoven together, come to form a scriptural mosaic—a truly "new context"—and help bring into relief the spiritual sense of the passage.

The third and final step of this Marian method is a "keeping through" of the Word of God in faith.[8] In this step, the scripture passage is "re-read in the light of this new context." At times this may require abandoning preconceived notions in order to reform them according to newly acquired insights. Withal, despite experiencing an initial obscurity, the path indicated by the prior steps is adhered to and faithfully followed. Thus, do we endeavor to allow the Word of God to be revealed, fully magnified, such that every word might contribute to and accord with the final interpretation. The indispensable principles to be followed here, to be sure, are prayer, reverence, discovery and wonder. All understanding is a gift from God.

---

[6] Cf. *suntereo*, *Lk* 2:19.

[7] Cf. *sumballo*, *Lk* 2:19.

[8] Cf. *diatereo*, *Lk* 2:51.

By way of illustration, we may envision the spiritual sense as being circumscribed, as it were, by each distinct word of the passage. As each word on this perimeter becomes more fully "opened" or revealed by the grace of the Holy Spirit, we come to glimpse in part, and ultimately to behold in full, the radiant center which is this spiritual sense. Such is the nature of the Word of God. Received by the finite intellect as diverse rays of light in its words and concepts, these stream forth from the one, true Light, the Word Incarnate, Jesus Christ.[9]

Word Study

I. *Kecharitoméne* and the Immaculate Conception

Kecharitoméne is a verb, a perfect (or past) participle. As such, it indicates an action "perfectly" completed. Thus, *the grace that* Kecharitoméne *signifies must have already been bestowed on Mary at the time of the Archangel's greeting.* This is an extremely important doctrinal point. St. Gabriel cannot here be referring to the grace of the Divine Maternity, as this grace is completed or "perfected" only with her consent. Only with her *Fiat* does the Immaculate become the Mother of God. And so, then, we must ask, what grace does the Archangel Gabriel attribute to Mary, a grace previously—and "perfectly"—accomplished?

Kecharitoméne: a Personal and "Actual" Name

First we note that the form of greeting, curiously, is neither a noun nor an adjective. Rather, a verb serves as the personal address of her name or title. The Archangel, sent and inspired by God with this greeting, had no better way of identifying the Immaculate than with the dynamism of action. Such is the angelic intuition of her essence. Moreover, "it is God himself who, through his angel as intermediary, greets Mary" (*CCC* 2676). Mary's very being is

---

9   This method should typically result in what we may call a *convergence of witnesses,* that is, recurring and intersecting themes from disparate words (i.e., various points on the perimeter), all of which inexorably converge upon the same spiritual sense. Like road signs, these provide some confirmation that the interpretation we are following is indeed authentic.

identified by act, and nothing less than a divine act. She is most beautifully named, from and by Heaven, as she who has been "fully-graced."

In light of this, we come to understand more clearly the words of Our Lady at Lourdes, "I am the Immaculate Conception." For here again Mary's person is identified by an act: she *is* a conception, the Immaculate Conception. Now, conception indicates a beginning or origin. It is the very movement from potency to act realized. And so, fully in accord with the mind of the Church, we may rightly associate these two personal and *actual* identifications: *Kecharitoméne* and the Immaculate Conception.

Kecharitoméne and Eternal Predestination

Another similarity of the terms *Kecharitoméne* and "conception" plunges us into the tremendous mystery of predestination. *The Oxford Dictionary of Philosophy* defines "conceive" as "to hold in the mind, or form an idea of something." Our Lady as the Immaculate Conception was held, so to speak, in the mind of God from all eternity. The Church teaches: "God, by one and the same decree, had established the origin of Mary and the Incarnation of Divine Wisdom."[10] This "origin" of Mary surely refers to her Immaculate Conception. Moreover, from the scriptural perspective, the Church also teaches: "As *full of grace* she has been eternally present in the mystery of Christ."[11] Yet again, a theological convergence of the Immaculate Conception and *Kecharitoméne* is evident.

II. *Kecharitoméne* and the Mediatrix of All Graces

Kecharitoméno in the Old Testament

The closest parallel in all of Sacred Scripture to the Virgin's title "full of grace" occurs in the Book of Sirach (18:17).

> [15] *My son, blemish not thy good deeds, neither use uncomfortable words when thou givest any thing.*
> [16] *Shall not the dew assuage the heat?*

---

[10] Bl. Pius IX, *Ineffabillis Deus.*

[11] St. John Paul II, *Redemptoris Mater,* 19.

so is a word better than a gift.
¹⁷ Lo, is not a word better than a gift?
but both are with a gracious [kecharitoméno] man.

First, it should be noted that the context is an exhortation to be without *blemish:* that is, how one ought to be immaculate in good deeds. Next, St. John Chrysostom explains for us how a word may excel a gift, insofar as one's words become the gift: "For it is possible even with words to give alms."[12] Last, let us consider that the *gracious man* here prefigured is a type of Jesus Christ, *full of grace and truth:* He who is Himself Gift and Word. The passage in comparing "word" with "gift," contrasts that which is spoken versus that which is given. Yet both find an ultimate unity only in the "gracious (*kecharitoméno*) man," Jesus Christ, in whom Word is Gift and Gift is Word.

From the Old Testament let us now return to the New, to the Annunciation, with a broadened perspective of the term "full of grace." The Blessed Virgin Mary, as *Kecharitoméne (fully-graced)*, is now understood to have been blessed with the same unity of word and gift as her Son. By way of illustration, we need only look to the following scene of the Visitation, as St. Elizabeth cries out: *As soon as the voice of thy salutation sounded in my ears, the infant in my womb leaped for joy (Lk 1:44).* The very word of Mary's greeting has become gift, the gift of sanctifying grace for St. John the Baptist: for the Word Incarnate in her womb has now also become her word, and grace is conceived thereby.[13] In this light, we see how at the Incarnation the Divine Word became as a creature, and the word of a creature became as though divine.

Echarítosen in the New Testament

The closest parallel of *Kecharitoméne* as a verb occurs in *Ephesians* 1:6.

---

12 *Homily 51, Comm. Mt* 15:1.

13 "St. Justin Martyr, in his dialogue with Trypho, uses a striking expression; he tells us that Mary, receiving the message of the angel, conceived 'faith and joy' (100, 5: *PG* 6, 710). In the Mother of Jesus, faith demonstrated its fruitfulness" (*Lumen fidei*, 58).

As he chose us in him before the foundation of the world,
that we should be holy and unspotted in his sight in charity.
⁵ Who hath predestinated us unto the adoption of children
through Jesus Christ unto himself:
according to the purpose of his will:
⁶ Unto the praise of the glory of his grace,
in which he hath graced [echarítosen] us, in his beloved Son.

Again, like the passage above from *Sirach*, the immediate context pertains to being "without blemish" (v. 4), which is simply another way of saying "immaculate." And again, like the magisterial teachings cited above, *Ephesians* here concerns the predestination of man. And so, in this one passage of Scripture we discover two significant and recurring associations: namely, being "immaculate" and predestination. What's going on here?

In order to discover a fuller sense of *echarítosen* in verse 6, we would do well first to look to the architecture of the passage. There exists in *Ephesians* 1 a remarkably strong parallel between vv. 4–6 and vv. 11–12 (cf. Table 1).[14] And the most important correlation to focus on is that the "has graced" (*echarítosen*) of v. 6 corresponds to—and may therefore reasonably be qualified by—the "before hoped" (*proelpízō*) of v. 12.

Before proceeding further, it seems opportune to review what has been said thus far regarding the dimensions of the word *Kecharitoméne*. Both Old Testament and New Testament parallels point to the notion of being "without blemish" (*Sir* 18:15 and *Eph* 1:4). The Old Testament furnished us with a Christological perspective, "the gracious man" of *Sirach*, in whom gift unites with word. Then, this same union of grace and word was seen in the person of the Mother of God during the Visitation, through her word of greeting and the consequent sanctification of St. John the Baptist. Now, in the New Testament of *Ephesians* the focus becomes the Christian and on how Christ *has graced us*. And, finally, our present conclusion is—given the parallel structure of *Ephesians* 1—that Christ *has graced us* precisely with a prevenient

---

[14] A demonstration of the validity of this parallel structure goes beyond the scope of this brief study and thus will be left to the judgment of the reader.

hope, namely, the "before hope" (*proelpizō*) of *Ephesians* 1:12. Such has been our inquiry of *Kecharitomẻne* thus far.

Table 1: Architecture: *Ephesians* 1:4–6 and 11–12

I. Chosen and Predestined in Christ, according to His will.	I. Called by Lot and Predestined in Christ, according to His will.
⁴ As he **chose** us in him before the foundation of the world, that we should be holy and unspotted in his sight in charity. ⁵ Who hath **predestinated** us unto the adoption of children through Jesus Christ unto Himself: according to the purpose of **his will**:	¹¹ In whom we also are **called by lot**, being **predestinated** according to the purpose of him who worketh all things according to the counsel of **his will**
eklegomai, **to select** *proorizō*, **predestine** *thelēma*, **will**	*kleroo*, **chosen by lot** *proorizō*, **predestine** *thelēma*, **will**
II. The Praise of Glory, *Having been graced* in the Beloved.	II. The Praise of Glory, *Hoping before* in Christ.
⁶ Unto the **praise** of the **glory** of his grace, in which he **hath graced** us, in his beloved son.	¹² That we may be unto the **praise** of his **glory**: we who **before hoped** in Christ.
epainos, **praise** *doxa*, **glory** *charitoō*, **to grace**	*epainos*, **praise** *doxa*, **glory** *proelpizō*, **to hope before**

But now what can be said of this prevenient hope? What does it mean for the Christian to "hope before"? The word *proelpizō* itself remains enigmatic, insofar as it occurs only in *Ephesians* and nowhere else in Sacred Scripture. Still, help may be afforded by a concordant verse in *Colossians* 1:5. Here the two passages are placed side-by-side.

... we who **before hoped** in Christ. In whom you also, after you had **heard** the **word of truth** (the **gospel** of your salvation). (*Eph* 1:12–13)	For the **hope** that is laid up for you in heaven, which you have [**before**] **heard** in the **word of the truth** of the **gospel**. (*Col* 1:5)

Both passages evidence five concordances: to hope, to hear, word, truth and gospel. And these, moreover, all occur in the same sequence. The only difference between them is that whereas *Ephesians* speaks of a "before hoped," *Colossians* speaks of a "before heard" (*proakouō*). And this prevenient hearing, akin to its counterpart, occurs but once in all of Sacred Scripture. And so, our investigation of *Kecharitoméne*, itself an absolutely unique verb, has yielded two other absolutely singular verbs, both of which are prefixed by *pro* (or *fore-*). Consequently, the little help gained by this tangential inquiry seems, at present, to be simply a reemphasis of the idea of prevenience.

Let us now return to our source text of *Ephesians* 1:6 to regain some perspective. St. John Chrysostom writes beautifully on how *echarítosen* pertains to the grace of justification.

"Which He freely bestowed on us," he says. He does not say, "Which He has graciously given us," (*echarísato*) but, "wherein He has shown grace to us," (*echarítosen*). That is to say, He has not only released us from our sins, but has also made us meet objects of His love. It is as though one were to take a leper, wasted by distemper and disease, by age, and poverty, and famine, and were to turn him all at once into a graceful youth, surpassing all mankind in beauty, shedding a bright luster from his cheeks, and eclipsing the sun-beams with the glances of his eyes; and then were to set him in the very flower of his age, and after that array him in purple and a diadem and all the attire of royalty. It is thus that God has arrayed and adorned this soul of ours, and clothed it with beauty, and rendered it an object of His delight and love. Such a soul angels desire to look into, yes, archangels and all the holy ones. Such grace has He shed over us, so dear has He rendered us to Himself. "The King," says the Psalmist, "shall greatly desire your beauty" (*Ps* 45:11).[15]

St. Thomas concurs that *echaritosen* refers to the bestowal of sanctifying grace, the grace of justification which makes one pleasing to God.[16]

Now, the notion of prevenience is prevalent in the Church's theology of justification. For example, the *Catechism* (1124) teaches: "The Church's faith precedes the faith of the believer, who is invited to adhere to it." And such precedence occurs not only within salvation history but also within the human heart. Hear the Council of Trent on "The Manner of Preparation" for justification:

> Now, they [the adults] are disposed to that justice when, aroused and aided by divine grace, receiving faith by **hearing** (*Rom* 10:17), they are moved freely toward God, believing to be true what has been divinely revealed and promised, especially that the sinner is justified by God by his grace, through the redemption that is in Christ Jesus (*Rom* 3:24); and when, understanding themselves to be sinners, they, by turning themselves from the fear of divine justice, by which they are salutarily aroused, to consider the mercy of God, are raised to **hope**, trusting that God will be propitious to them for Christ's sake; and they begin to love Him as the fountain of all justice, and on that account are moved against sin by a certain hatred and detestation, that is, by that repentance that must be performed before baptism[17]; finally, when they resolve to receive baptism, to begin a new life and to keep the commandments of God.[18]

Let us note carefully the contours of this prevenient grace. Primarily a faith received "by hearing," it subsequently arouses to hope. And we recall that such are precisely the two actions previously discovered in *Colossians* 1:5 (*proakouō*) and *Ephesians* 1:12 (*proelpizō*). In brief, our New Testament inquiry of *Kecharitoméne* has underscored not only the call of the Christian

---

15 *Comm. Ephesians*, 1.

16 Cf. *Comm. Eph.*, c. 1, lecture 2.

17 Cf. Sess. XIV, c. 4.

18 Sess. VI, c. 6.

to be immaculate, "without blemish," but has also strongly indicated the role of a prevenient grace of hope toward that end in the process of justification.

Conclusion

Kecharitoméne is the divinely inspired title of the Immaculate. Like the Holy Name of Jesus ("God saves"), it signifies both identity and mission. Part I of this study confirmed the former, noting the congruence of being and act in *Kecharitoméne* and the self-identification of Lourdes, "I am the Immaculate Conception." Part II then immersed us in the latter, the mission of *Kecharitoméne* (again, we recall that it is a verb). And here we discovered the term's correlation with a prevenient grace of hope in the process of justification. Now, given that "We are in justice bound to recognize the hidden influence of Mary in obtaining the gift of faith and its salutary cultivation" (Leo XIII, *Adiutricem populi,* 1895), a concerted and vigorous effort is called for in future studies to explore this theme within the Marian biblical texts. For the moment, we suffice merely to begin a response to our initial query, thus greeting her from afar: Who are you, *Kecharitoméne?* You are the Immaculate Mediatrix of All Graces.

WORD STUDY: *DIALOGISOMAI*

Abstract

The following comparative word study on the usage of the Greek word dialogisomai *in the New Testament offers a "strong scriptural indication" of the singular privilege of the Immaculate Conception of the Blessed Virgin Mary.*

Introduction

The Greek verb *dialogisomai* ("to reason," "to think," or "to deliberate") occurs in eight different contexts throughout the New Testament. This word is of special interest to Mariology because it is found in the Annunciation text, where St. Luke employs *dialogisomai* to portray that most pivotal of all moments in salvation history, when the Immaculate Virgin Mary pauses to reflect upon the Archangel Gabriel's greeting:

> *"[She] kept pondering what manner of greeting this might be."*[1]

Upon surveying the seven remaining usages of *dialogisomai* in the New Testament, it becomes evident that everyone else who attempts to reason in this way, whether it be the apostles, the chief priests and elders, or the scribes—indeed, all men— universally do not arrive at the truth of things via *dialogisomai*, but rather fall into error and, consequently, into sin. In other words, a certain ubiquitous frustration, or even futility, to the human faculty of reason accompanies the verb *dialogisomai*. Now, the sole exception to this etymological trend is seen in the Immaculate Virgin Mary at the Annunciation. Her reason does not fail her at the critical moment of discernment and decision, even though she is greatly "troubled" by Gabriel's greeting because of her humility. Still, she does not waver in giving her assent because she is the Immaculate and as such is "wholly borne by God's grace."[2] However, juxtaposed to the

---

[1] *Lk* 1:29.

[2] *CCC* 490.

Immaculate Virgin Mary at the Annunciation—and this is what is most astonishing—the seven remaining passages in which we find *dialogisomai* stand in direct correspondence to the seven capital sins.

Word Study

The following seven passages in which *dialogisomai* occurs have been classified below according to their specific correspondence to a capital sin. The English translation of *dialogisomai* has been italicized.

1. "**Pride** is undue self-esteem or self-love, which seeks attention and honor."[3] As the Apostles adequately demonstrate in the following passage, pride often manifests itself as "a desire to surpass one's equals."[4]

   > And they came to Capharnaum. When He was at home, He asked them, "What were you *arguing* about on the way?" But they kept silence, for on the way they had discussed with one another which of them was the greatest.[5]

2. **Avarice** is "a disordered inclination or desire for pleasure or possessions."[6] The covetous man in the following parable is driven by an inordinate fear of losing his possessions.

   > And He said to them, "Take heed and guard yourselves from all covetousness, for a man's life does not consist in the abundance of his possessions." But He spoke a parable to them, saying, "The land of a certain rich man brought forth abundant crops. And he began *to take thought within himself*, saying, 'What shall I do, for I have no room to store my crops?' And he said, 'I will do this: I will pull down my barns and build larger ones, and there I will store up all my grain and my goods. And I will say to my soul, Soul, you have

---

3   *CCC* glossary.

4   Attwater, *A Catholic Dictionary.*

5   *Mk* 9:32–33.

6   *CCC* glossary.

many good things laid up for many years; take your ease, eat, drink, be merry.'"[7]

3. **Envy** is "resentment or sadness at another's good fortune, and the desire to have it for oneself."[8] It was out of envy that Cain killed his brother Abel. Here in the Parable of the Wicked Tenants, the vinedressers follow in their father's murderous footsteps.

> But the vinedressers, on seeing him, *argued* with one another saying, "This is the heir; let us kill him, that the inheritance may become ours."[9]

4. **Wrath (or Anger)** is an inordinate desire for revenge over injustices (real or imaginary) done to us. Here, after Jesus' powerful demonstration of righteous (or "zealous") anger in the Cleansing of the Temple, the chief priests and elders react with indignation, which is one of the six "daughters" of anger listed by St. Thomas Aquinas.[10]

> And when He had come into the temple, the chief priests and elders of the people came to Him as He was teaching, and said, "By what authority do You do these things? And who gave You this authority?" Jesus answered and said to them, "I also will ask you one question, and if you answer Me this, I in turn will tell you by what authority I do these things. Whence was the baptism of John? From heaven or from men?" But they began to *argue* among themselves…[11]

5. **Lust** is an inordinate desire for sexual pleasure. It is also "the chief cause of lack of rectitude in the reason."[12] That is to say, lust, more than any other vice, brings about error. The following passage provides a link with this capital sin in the figure of the adulterous King Herod, whose lust ultimately caused the

---

7   *Lk* 12:15–19.

8   *CCC* glossary.

9   *Lk* 20:14.

10 Cf. *ST* II-II Q. 158, a. 7.

11 *Mt* 21:23–25; cf. *Lk* 20:1–5.

12 *ST* II-II, Q. 55, a. 8, obj. 1.

death of St. John the Baptist. Herod's lust was also—one may infer—the "chief cause" of his erroneous belief that Jesus was the Baptist come back to life. Here, the people are mistaken in a similar vein by confusing St. John the Baptist for the Christ.

> Now as the people were in expectation, and all were *wondering* in their hearts about John, whether perhaps he might be the Christ... But Herod the tetrarch, being reproved by him concerning Herodias, his brother's wife, and concerning all the evil things that Herod had done, crowned all this by shutting up John in prison.[13]

6. **Gluttony** is defined as "overindulgence in food or drink."[14] It may be manifested by being overly preoccupied with food or even by an obsessive anticipation of one's next meal, as the Apostles demonstrate here.

> And they began to *argue* among themselves, saying, "We have no bread." But Jesus knowing this, said to them, "Why do you *argue* because you have no bread? Do you not yet perceive, nor understand? Is your heart still blinded? Though you have eyes do you not see, and though you have ears do you not hear? And do you not remember? ... How is it that you do not yet understand?"[15]

7. **Sloth (or Acedia)** is "a culpable lack of physical or spiritual effort."[16] Archbishop Fulton Sheen notes that it is manifested in laziness, procrastination, idleness, indifference and nonchalance. In the following passage, the four friends of the paralytic are anything but slothful, having climbed up to the roof of the house where Jesus is in order to lower their friend at the feet of the Divine Physician. However, the scribes, who are seated comfortably nearby, may be charged with sloth on two counts: (1) a "lack of physical effort" in that they witness the whole scene as it unfolds *sitting down*, not offering even a modicum of help, and (2) a "lack of spiritual effort" in that they are not

---

13 *Lk* 3:15, 19.

14 *CCC* glossary.

15 *Mk* 8:16, 17, 21; cf. *Mt* 16:7, 8.

16 *CCC* glossary.

moved to compassion for the paralytic, and neither are they moved to an act of faith in Jesus, despite witnessing the miracle.

> And Jesus, seeing their faith, said to the paralytic, "Son, your sins are forgiven you." Now some of the scribes were sitting there and *reasoning* in their hearts, "Why does this man speak thus? He blasphemes. Who can forgive sins but only God?"[17]

Conclusion

In view of the preceding comparative word study, the New Testament usage of *dialogisomai* indicates two significant findings:

1. The ultimate futility of human reason without the help of grace, due to original sin and its specific effect of the darkening of the intellect (traditionally called *ignorance*).

2. The absolutely singular and superior reasoning capacity of the Immaculate, who alone successfully arrives at the truth of things—vis-à-vis the illumination of supernatural faith—and is identified by the Archangel Gabriel as "full of grace."

Therefore, a detailed study of *dialogisomai* in the New Testament provides a *strong scriptural indication* of the absolutely singular privilege of the Immaculate Conception: that is, Our Lady's faculty of reason stands alone as having never been darkened by original sin and ignorance.

---

17 *Mk* 2:5–7; cf. *Lk* 5:21, 22.

WORD STUDY: *PARALAMBANO*

The four Marian dogmas have their clear foundation in Sacred Scripture. But it is there like a seed that grows and bears fruit.

—Joseph Cardinal Ratzinger [1]

Abstract

The following scriptural word-study of the Greek verbs paralambano *and* lambano *provides a "scriptural support" of the Dogma of the Perpetual Virginity of the Immaculate Virgin Mary. By extension, its conclusions point to a prior vow of virginity on the part of St. Joseph.*

Introduction

Paralambano: *an entirely exceptional marriage*

The expression "to take" a wife occurs in Sacred Scripture 111 times: 103 in the Old Testament (LXX) and eight in the New Testament.[2] The phrase is of special significance to Mariology because it depicts the final stage of marriage between St. Joseph and the Blessed Virgin Mary. As such, these words can tell us much about the nature of their marital union. We find the expression used twice in the account of the Annunciation to St. Joseph:

An angel of the Lord appeared to him in a dream, saying, "Do not be afraid, Joseph, son of David, **to take to you** *Mary your wife,*

---

[1] Joseph Cardinal Ratzinger with Vittorio Messori, *The Ratzinger Report* (San Francisco: Ignatius Press, 1985), 107.

[2] Cf. *Gen* 4:19; 6:3; 11:29; 12:19; 16:3; 20:2, 3; 21:21; 24:3, 4, 7, 37, 38, 40, 51, 67; 25:1, 20; 26:34; 27:46; 28:1, 2, 6, 6, 9; 29:23; 30:9; 31:50; 34:4, 16, 21; 36:2; 38:6; *Ex* 6:20, 23, 25; *Lev* 18:18; 20:14, 21; 21:7, 13, 14; *Num* 12:1, 1; *Deut* 20:7; 21:11; 22:13, 14, 30 [23:1]; 24:3, 4, 5; 25:5, 7; 28:30; *Jgs* 3:6; 14:2, 3; 15:6; 19:1; 21:22, 23; *Ruth* 1:4; 4:13; 1 *Sam* 25:39, 40, 43; 2 *Sam* 3:14; 5:13; 12:9, 10; 20:3; 1 *Kings* 4:15; 11:1; 16:31; 1 *Chron* 2:19, 21; 4:18; 7:15; 14:3; 2 *Chron* 11:18, 20; 13:21; 24:3; 1 *Esdras* 8:36; *Ezra* 2:61; 10:44; *Neh* 6:18; 7:63 13:25; *Tob* 4:12, 12, 12, 13; 7:13; 8:7; *Jer* 16:1; 29:6, 6 [36:6, 6]; *Ezek* 44:22; *Dan* 13:2; *Hos* 1:2, 3; *Mt* 1:20, 24; *Mk* 12:19, 20, 21; *Lk* 20:28, 29, 31.

*for that which is begotten in her is of the Holy Spirit... So Joseph,
arising from sleep, did as the angel of the Lord had commanded
him, and **took unto him** his wife. (Mt 1:20, 24)*

The specific verb employed here by St. Matthew is *paralambano,*
"to take to one's side." It is a remarkable choice of vocabulary by
the Evangelist in light of the fact that *paralambano* is never once
used in a marriage context anywhere else in all of Sacred Scripture.
Rather, both the Old and New Testaments exclusively reserve the
verb *lambano* ("to take") for this purpose. For example, whenever
we read of a man (or his proxy) "taking" a wife in the Old
Testament, in every instance—103 times in all—the Greek word
is always, without fail, *lambano.* Never do we find *paralambano*
in this context. Abram, Isaac, Ishmael, Esau, Aaron, Samson,
David, Boaz, Tobit, Hosea and Joachim are but a small sampling
of Old Testament husbands who "took" wives in precisely this way
(i.e., via *lambano*).[3] The New Testament, moreover, confirms this
etymological motif. Here again we also find—the sole exception
being St. Joseph—that *lambano* is employed exclusively for the
"taking" of a wife.[4] In this way, then, we come to discover that the
occurrence of *paralambano* in *Matthew* 1:20, 24 is utterly unique in
all of Sacred Scripture. That is, St. Joseph alone "takes to himself"
his bride, the Virgin Mary, in an entirely exceptional fashion.

Therefore, the question necessarily arises: What's going on here?
Why this odd and unexpected vocabulary? Why this inspired
anomaly?

Method

A distinctively Marian approach to biblical theology: "keeping the Word"

On the doctrinal level our query is, of course, a foregone
conclusion. The Faith readily affords us the certainty that the
marriage between St. Joseph and Our Lady was indeed singular:

---

3 Cf. *Gen* 11:29; 24:67; 21:21; 26:34; *Ex* 6:23; 2 *Sam* 5:13; 12:9; *Ruth* 4:13; *Tob* 8:7; *Hos*
1:2; *Dan* 13:2

4 Cf. *Mk* 12:19, 20, 21; *Lk* 20:28, 29, 31.

both intended and thus consented to live in perpetual continence and so never physically consummated their marriage.[5] Nevertheless, our present task is to concern ourselves only with what Sacred Scripture tells us about the matter. Such a course of study, we hope, will be of some value to our separated brethren, to those whose faith depends solely on the written Word of God.

Now, to return to our question, but with an explicitly "scriptural tack," we must endeavor to explore the depth of meaning inherent in these two key words: *paralambano* and *lambano*. The question, when viewed through this lens, sharpens into focus as: Why did the Holy Spirit inspire *paralambano* in *Matthew* 1:20, 24 in lieu of an otherwise universal predilection for *lambano* in a marriage context?

Let us first consider that each particular word of Scripture, being inspired by the Holy Spirit and issuing forth through human agency, carries within itself as does a seed, an innate potential, a profound significance—what is perhaps best termed a *resonance of meaning*. That is to say, intrinsic to the Word of God exists a depth of meaning that is only fully revealed and comprehended when the part (i.e., this particular usage) is viewed in light of the whole (i.e., how this particular word is used throughout the entirety of Sacred Scripture). Such a method presupposes, surprisingly, that there is a certain legitimacy, albeit limited, to the assertion that the Word itself interprets the Word.

Let us now consider that this theological method is essentially Marian. It first entails a gathering together of disparate scriptural passages, each of which contains the desired word of study. Our Lady herself exemplifies this "keeping together" (*suntereo*), or gathering-up of words in her Heart.[6] Next, a prayerful contemplation of these scriptures in concert can yield a deeper understanding—a *resonance of meaning*—in which an individual scriptural passage is seen in light of the context of the collected whole. The Immaculate Virgin, "who kept all the great things the Almighty had done and treasured

---

5 From this belief of the faithful arose the concept of the "Josephite marriage" in the life of the Church.

6 Cf. *Lk* 2:19.

them in her heart," again exemplifies this contemplative "keeping through" (*diatereo*) of the Word of God, despite suffering its initial obscurity.[7] The Venerable St. Bede opens a valuable "window" into Our Lady's interior in this regard:

"The Virgin, whether she understood or whether she could not yet understand, equally laid up all things in her heart for reflection and diligent examination... She pondered upon both His divine words and works, so that nothing that was said or done by Him was lost upon her, but as the Word itself was before in her womb, so now she conceived the ways and words of the same, and in a manner nursed them in her heart. And while indeed she thought upon one thing at the time, another she wanted to be more clearly revealed to her; and this was her constant rule and law through her whole life."[8]

Results

Using this distinctively Marian approach to Sacred Scripture— contemplating the Word from within the Heart of the Immaculate—we come to discover two noteworthy associations to the verbs *lambano* and *paralambano* in their literal sense.

1. *Lambano* indicates a consummated marriage

A close study of *lambano* in a marriage context in both the Old and New Testaments reveals a significant association with consummation. At times this is made quite explicit with the phrase, "he went in to her."[9] Other times it is implied contextually: for example, via the presence (or absence) of the "tokens of virginity,"[10] nakedness,[11] or in certain condemnable violations of the sixth commandment.[12] Most often, however, the association is indicated

---

7   Cf. CCC 2599; *Lk* 2:51; *Dan* 7:28.

8   *Catena Aurea, Lk* 2:51.

9   Cf. *Gen* 6:2–5; 16:3–4; 29:23; 30:9; 38:6–9; *Deut* 21:11–13; 25:5; *Jgs* 15:1 (inclusive of 14:2, 3, 3, 8; 15:6); *Ruth* 4:13; 1 *Kgs* 11:1; 1 *Chron* 2:21; cf. also *Gen* 31:50.

10 Cf. *Deut* 22:13, 14.

11 Cf. *Lev* 18:18.

12 Cf. *Gen* 12:19; 20:2, 3; *Gen* 34:4; *Lev* 20:14, 21; 21:7, 13, 14; *Deut* 22:30; 24:3, 4, 5; 2 *Sam* 12:9, 10; *Tob* 8:7.

by the presence of children as the blessed fruit of a consummated marriage,[13] or, conversely, through their lamented absence due to the curse of barrenness.[14] Overall, then, for the majority of cases (~75%) in which we find *lambano* employed in a marriage context, we find that a consummated marriage is unambiguously implied.[15]

2. *Paralambano* indicates a relation of kinship

Paralambano, on the other hand, indicates none of the above. Again, we recall that it is never even used in a marriage context. What it does clearly indicate, however, in the Old Testament is a relation of kinship. This relation is often within one's own family,[16] people,[17] or nation.[18] Indeed, the verb *paralambano* in the Old Testament appears to be predicated entirely upon ethnicity. In other words, it is used predominantly either between Jews themselves[19] or between Gentiles themselves.[20] And here it may truly be said, "Never the twain shall meet"—at least not via *paralambano.* Indeed, to do so arouses a vehement and diving repugnance.[21] Thus, in diverse ways, the notion of kinship appears as something altogether intrinsic to the verb *paralambano* in the Old Testament.

---

[13] Cf. *Gen* 4:19; 24:7, 40, 51, 67; 25:1, 20–22; 28:1, 2, 6, 6, 9; 36:2; *Ex* 6:20, 23, 25; 2 *Sam* 5:13; 1 *Chron* 2:19, 21; 4:18; 7:15; 14:3; 2 *Chron* 11:18, 20; 13:21; 24:3; 1 *Esdras* 8:36; *Ezra* 10:44; *Neh* 13:25; *Tob* 4:12, 12, 12, 13; *Jer* 16:1; 29:6, 6; *Hos* 1:2, 3. Cf. also, the raising up children for one's deceased brother: *Dt* 25:7; *Mk* 12:19, 20, 22; *Lk* 20:28, 29, 30.

[14] Cf. *Gen* 11:29.

[15] The remaining passages do not in any way contra-indicate consummation, but rather simply do not positively indicate it within the immediate context.

[16] Cf. *Gen* 22:3; 31:23; **45:18; 47:2;** *Song* 8:2; *Jer* 32:7 [39:7]. The citations in bold pertain to *adelphoi* or "brethren."

[17] Cf. *Jos* 4:2; *Jgs* 9:43; 2 *Chron* 25:11.

[18] Cf. *Jer* 49:1, 2 [30:1, 2].

[19] Cf. *Gen* 22:3; 31:23; 45:18; 47:2; *Jos* 4:2; *Jgs* 9:43; 11:5; 2 *Chron* 25:11; *Jer* 32:7 [39:7]; 49:1, 2 [30:1, 2]; 2 *Macc* 5:5

[20] Cf. *Num* 22:41; 23:14, 27, 28; *Dan* 5:31; 1 *Macc* 3:37; 4:1.

[21] Cf. *Jer* 49:1 [30]:1. Two other Jew-Gentile interactions via *paralambano* occur only in the context of prisoners-of-war (cf. *Jdt* 6:20; 1 *Macc* 5:23).

Evidence of the New Testament

The New Testament, moreover, confirms this reading of the Old.[22] We read in the Prologue of St. John's Gospel: *He came unto His own, and His own received Him not* (paralambano); *but as many as received Him* (lambano), *He gave power to become children of God.*[23] Herein we find an "archetypal usage" of our terms, inasmuch as *paralambano* and *lambano* are so clearly juxtaposed, set in relief as it were. First we note that *paralambano* yet again conveys a relation of kinship: Jesus' own are, of course, His own kinsmen, fellow Israelites who lived in eager expectation of the Messiah and, yet, failed to receive His coming by faith. *Lambano*, on the other hand, here suggests a more intimate receiving of Jesus by faith, and, remarkably, still retains a correlation with procreation even in its spiritual sense.

Next, we ought to consider that, in establishing the New Covenant, Jesus has radically transformed the very idea of kinship.[24] No longer do ethnic lines divide and alienate peoples in the Kingdom of God.[25] And so, the usage of *paralambano* in the New Testament reflects this new reality, corresponds to this new economy of grace. Although still retaining a residual link with the OT notion of kinship as family[26] and nation,[27] the distinctive characteristic of *paralambano* in the NT—its resplendent hallmark,

---

[22] In the New Testament *paralambano* is used both in a personal sense – i.e., a "taking" or "receiving" of another person (cf. *Mt* 1:20, 24; 2:13, 14, 20, 21; 4:5, 8; 12:45; 17:1; 18:16; 20:17; 24:40, 41; 26:37; 27:27; *Mk* 4:36; 5:40; 9:2; 10:32; 14:33; *Lk* 9:10, 28; 11:26; 17:34, 35, 35; 18:31; *Jn* 1:11; 14:3; 19:16; *Acts* 15:39; 16:33; 21:24, 26, 32; 23:18; *Col* 2:6), as well as in a conceptual sense – i.e., a "taking" or "receiving" of some abstract reality (cf. *Mk* 7:4; 1 *Cor* 11:23; 15:1, 3; *Gal* 1:9, 12; *Phil* 4:9; 1 *Thess* 2:13; 4:1; 2 *Thess* 3:6; *Heb* 12:28). We shall limit our study to the former, as this pertains to the literal sense of *paralambano* in *Mt* 1:20, 24. The latter conceptual sense also pertains to the interpretation of the passage, but in its spiritual sense: viz., with the Immaculate comes the transmission of the Faith (cf. 1 *Cor* 11:23; 15:1, 3; *Gal* 1:9, 12; *Phil* 4:9; *Col* 2:6; 1 *Thess* 2:13; 4:1; 2 *Thess* 3:6), an immanence of the Kingdom of God by grace (cf. *Heb* 12:28).

[23] *Jn* 1:11–12.

[24] Cf. *Jn* 19:25–27.

[25] Cf. *Rom* 10:12; 1 *Cor* 12:13; *Col* 3:11.

[26] Cf. *Mt* 1:20, 24; 2:13, 14, 20, 21.

[27] Cf. *Acts* 21:32.

so to speak—now appears as the Christian family, our communion with and in Christ Jesus.[28] It is with and in His Sacred Humanity that all may truly be accounted "brethren," forming one Body in Christ: that he might make the two in himself into one new man, making peace.[29] For example, St. Paul, the Apostle to the Gentiles, is found to *paralambano* with the Romans.[30] Such an explicit association between Jew and Gentile with this term is truly exceptional in Sacred Scripture.[31]

And so we find that the relation of kinship—with both its old and new significations—is positively indicated by *paralambano* in the vast majority of its usages throughout the Old and New Testaments.

Conclusion

St. Joseph intends paralambano and not lambano

Having thus examined the evidence of Scripture alone, we can now derive some conclusions, both reasoned and biblical, to the question: Why, precisely, did the Holy Spirit inspire *paralambano* in *Matthew* 1:20, 24 in lieu of an otherwise universal predilection for *lambano* in a marriage context?

First, we may affirm that St. Joseph "took to himself" the Blessed Virgin Mary to be his wife with the intentionality intrinsic to the verb *paralambano* in its literal sense: precisely, he took her to himself in a relation of kinship, specifically to live together as brother and sister. Such is the standard setting of the verb, such

---

[28] Cf. *Mt* 17:1; 18:16; 20:17; 26:37; *Mk* 4:36; 5:40; 9:2; 10:32; 14:33; *Lk* 9:10, 28; 18:31; *Jn* 14:3; *Acts* 15:39; *Col* 2:6.

[29] *Eph* 2:15.

[30] Cf. *Acts* 16:33; St. Paul effects the same for his nephew in *Acts* 23:18.

[31] Queen Esther, as a type of Our Lady, may be an exception to this rule (cf. *Est* 5:1 [15:5]). Jesus also is found to *paralambano* with the Gentiles, but it is they who "take" Him by force in order to crucify Him (cf. *Mt* 27:27; *Jn* 19:16). In this, Our Lord allowed Himself to be so completely "taken" (and not only by the Roman centurions, but even by the devil himself – cf. *Mt* 4:5, 8), that thereby we have been reconciled to God the Father through Him as adopted sons in the Son. This is the new paradigm of kinship for *paralambano* in the New Testament (cf. *Col* 2:6).

is the meaning of the angel's command (v. 20), and such is the perfect obedience of St. Joseph to the Divine Will (v. 24).

Second, it must also be admitted that St. Joseph expressly did *not* "take" the Blessed Virgin Mary to be his wife with the intentionality intrinsic to the verb *lambano* in its literal sense— that is, with an intention to physically consummate the marriage. The glaring omission of this normative verb for marriage leaves us with no other logical explanation that would adequately justify its curious absence—or better, its deliberate and inspired non-inclusion.

These two conclusions in tandem comprise a reasonable and, hopefully, scripturally-satisfying explanation for the atypical occurrence of *paralambano* in *Matthew* 1:20, 24. They are furthermore a scriptural support for the Dogma of the Perpetual Virginity of the Blessed Virgin Mary, and most pointedly, in its post-partum aspect—namely, that the Immaculate remained a virgin after the birth of Jesus and throughout her life.

Last, and by extension, *paralambano* points to a vow of virginity on the part of St. Joseph, as well. The angel's words, *Do not be afraid to take*, reveal that even prior to his discovery of Mary's pregnancy, such had been St. Joseph's original intention – i.e. *to take Mary as wife* in a state of consecrated virginity. We can deduce the following: if St. Joseph intended *to take* Mary, his wife, as brother and sister, then he intended to live lifelong chastity in marriage; if he thus intended a life of chastity, then St. Joseph may well have vowed chastity.

Apologia

The propitious outcome of our study should not surprise us. It is simply a validation of the divine congruence of two parallel currents of Revelation, namely, Tradition and Scripture. The Bible itself readily confirms the teachings of the Church that we already hold by faith: here, the Perpetual Virginity of the Blessed Virgin Mary. Hence, St. Paul exhorts us: "So then, brethren, stand firm and hold to the traditions which you were taught by us, either by word of mouth or by letter" (*2 Thess* 2:15).

Neither should this study be construed as eisegesis, a subjective reading into the biblical text of one's preconceived notions. It is rather a sincere attempt to adhere faithfully to the Word of God—in loving imitation of the Immaculate—wherever it may lead. Should the objection of eisegesis be raised to challenge the above conclusions, the burden of proof would necessarily fall to the honest objector to refute the scriptural correlations.

THE ACADEMY OF THE IMMACULATE

The Academy of the Immaculate, founded in 1992, is inspired by and based on a project of St. Maximilian Kolbe (never realized by the Saint because of his death by martyrdom at the age of 47, August 14, 1941). Among its goals the Academy seeks to promote at every level the study of the Mystery of the Immaculate Conception and the universal maternal mediation of the Virgin Mother of God, and to sponsor publication and dissemination of the fruits of this research in every way possible.

The Academy of the Immaculate is a non-profit religious-charitable organization of the Roman Catholic Church, incorporated under the laws of the Commonwealth of Massachusetts, with its central office at Our Lady's Chapel, POB 3003, New Bedford, MA 02741-3003.

AcademyoftheImmaculate.com

Special rates are available with 25% to 60% discount depending on the number of books, plus postage. For ordering books and further information on rates to book stores, schools and parishes: *Academy of the Immaculate, P.O. Box 3003, New Bedford, MA 02741*, Phone/FAX *(888)90.MARIA [888.90.62742]*, Email *academy@marymediatrix.com*. Quotations on bulk rates by the box, shipped directly from the printery, contact: *Academy of the Immaculate, P.O. Box 3003, New Bedford, MA 02741, (508)996-8274*, Email: *academy@marymediatrix.com*. *Web: academyoftheimmaculate.com*.